The

Roman Poet of Science

LUCRETIUS:

De Rerum Natura

Books by

Alban Dewes Winspear

THE GENESIS OF PLATO'S THOUGHT

with Tom Silverberg

WHO WAS SOCRATES?

The

Roman Poet of Science

LUCRETIUS:
De Rerum Natura

SET IN ENGLISH VERSE BY

Alban Dewes Winspear

New York

S·A·Russell·The Harbor Press

LIBRARY OF CONGRESS CATALOG CARD NUMBER 55–10272

COPYRIGHT © 1956 BY ALBAN DEWES WINSPEAR

First Printing December 1955

PRINTED AND BOUND IN THE U.S.A.
BY BOOK PRODUCTION CO. INC.

HOMINIS DILECTISSIMI

MORTUI PRAESENTIS

GULIELMI ELLERY LEONARD

IN PIAM MEMORIAM

D.D.

Preface

I HAVE WORKED on this translation of Lucretius into English verse with one good reason in mind—I wanted my favorite poet to be read. It seems to me that Lucretius has a great deal to say to the ordinary man in this generation, and in the current translations his message does not always get across. Munroe and Bailey, admirable though they are, are essentially scholar's translations, giving invaluable assistance to one who can read the Latin. Of the verse translations Mallock's seems Victorian and dated; Trevelyan stodgy; Leonard's (much as I value the intimacy of his friendship over nearly twenty years) is essentially a poet's translation, splendid in virtuosity and technique but hardly popular. Two translations have appeared since I completed this work (testifying to the profound interest which Lucretius excites in our generation). I have not yet had an opportunity to examine these.

It is my hope that many readers who have had little or no previous experience with Latin poetry or the history of ancient thought may find stimulus and excitement with Lucretius. Such people will face one great difficulty. Outmoded science is bound to be dull; in spots exciting only to the specialist. Lucretius does not escape this difficulty. In places he is difficult to follow, sometimes even dull. I suggest to new readers that they pick out famous passages where Lucretius really warms to his theme. A new reader should by all means try the introduction in *Book One,* and the sacrifice of Iphigeneia, and the poet's remarks on the fear of death, page 3 to top of page 9. In *Book*

Two, he should by all means read the introduction and the passage on the Great Mother of the Gods, pages 48 to 51 and 70 to 73. *Book Three* contains another splendid introduction in praise of Epicurus. From there the novice might go to the passages in which Lucretius tries to banish the fear of death, pages 126 to 136. In *Book Four,* after the introduction, the most famous passage is that in which Lucretius treats of love, pages 137 and 138, 178 to 188. The first few pages of *Book Five* are worth attention, pages 189 to 198, as are his arguments against the teleological view of the universe, pages 206 to 211. The account of the evolution of the universe, of man and of human institutions is most exciting, pages 221 to 225. After the introduction to *Book Six,* page 248 to top of page 252, the most famous passage in the book is the description of the plague at Athens, pages 294 to 299. A reader who has been stimulated by these preliminary explorations may now be ready to pursue the poet through his more difficult and duller moments.

The translator wishes to express his gratitude to the University of Wisconsin Press for permission to include the *Introduction* and the portions of the translation which have already appeared in the Wisconsin Anthology, *CLASSICS IN TRANSLATION* (University of Wisconsin Press, 1952).

He is also deeply indebted to the Librarian and staff of the University of British Columbia for making available the books he needed not only from their collection but also on inter-library loan.

Prof. H. T. Logan of the University of British Columbia has made a number of useful suggestions. My colleagues Miss Florence Pope and Mr. J. B. McLaren have been constant in their encouragement and have helped with their critical acumen.

Critics who are inclined to differ on matters of detail may perhaps take into account the fact that this work has been done in the busy interstices of the life of a teacher and administrator, for whom even ten minutes of undisturbed composition was difficult to find. TALIBUS VENIA DARI DEBET. The text followed has been in general

Bailey's. I owe much to his work and to the Smith-Leonard edition. I did not consult Leonard's verse translation while my work was in progress—deliberately. If there are echoes of Leonard's renderings, some chance remark or random quotation must have sunk into the deep well of memory.

ALBAN DEWES WINSPEAR

North Shore College,
North Vancouver,
March 6th, 1955

Contents

Contents

Introduction

IN MOST DEPARTMENTS of creative activity and artistic achievement, the Romans regarded themselves as inferior to the Greeks. In the field which Lucretius made his own—the poetical exposition of philosophical doctrine—they have no need to hang their heads in shame. For majesty of theme and subject matter, for sustained eloquence of exposition, for acuteness of philosophical insight and argumentation, for poetical imagery and musical cadence, and for the sheer enthusiasm of scientific passion, the Greeks—despite the philosophical contributions of Leucippus, Democritus, and Epicurus—produced nothing to rival Lucretius. Indeed I am not sure that, as regards all these qualities, Lucretius is not the greatest poet that ever lived.

Of Lucretius the man, apart from what we can infer from his great poem, we know singularly little. There is a legend of dubious validity and perhaps scandalous intent, that he was driven mad by a love philtre administered by a jealous woman, composed his poems in the lucid intervals of insanity, and died at the zenith of his ripened powers by his own hand. There is a debatable connection with Cicero (the renowned Marcus or his less famous brother) who may or may not have revised or edited the manuscript. At all events Marcus shows a proper appreciation, commendable in a philosophical opponent, of Lucretius' poem—"many flashes of genius and yet much art." The poem itself gives us a picture of an educated and aristocratic Roman familiar with the life of the *haut monde,* its luxurious palaces and country houses, its ostentation and vulgarity, its boredom with the banquet of externals. Yet Lucretius does not show much awareness of the exciting world around him—the crucial days of Rome's greatest civil wars. At one point he appeals to his goddess patron for peace,

> I cannot carry out this task of mine with mind at peace
> At such a crisis of my country's fate.

Negatively, the troubled times sent him to a creed of escape, a passionate opposition to the desire for wealth and power, a residence in what, following Lucretius, we have come to call the ivory tower.

Lucretius was before all things the poet of the scientific outlook, of philosophical materialism, of opposition to religion in creed and rite and myth. This opposition was his deepest passion; it gave rise to some of his most moving poetry. In his consideration of human evolution in general, this opposition leads him to some of his most majestic speculations—they are of the kind which we should now call anthropological—as to how this belief in the gods originated. It leads him to his most profound philosophical speculations. Against religion and a belief in the supernatural, which so many put forward to explain the origins of the universe and its government, he puts forward his atomic philosophy. And this opposition to religion, finally, accounts for his central ethical philosophy, his teaching about how man ought to live.

"There are two moments in Lucretius' zoology" writes Leonard, "that are notably Darwinian: the effect of organic adaptation and of domestication upon the preservation of the species; the survival value of swift legs, for instance, and of man's cooperation, both of which kept the earth stocked with animal life . . . [and] the Lucretian reiteration against teleology, that is, design in Nature, a favorite idea of Aristotle and of Lucretius' own much-scorned Stoics. Not only are there no Gods planning ahead from without; but Nature herself, he says, from within herself is not planning ahead: she merely grows, and things happen and particular functions develop out of what happens."*

The theory of special creation Lucretius sharply attacked, as well as any notion of design in nature. The earth is mortal, made without divine intervention and destined in its time to perish. In good naturalistic terms he explains what force and what cause started the various courses of the sun, the journeys of the moon, the position of the earth in the center of the universe, the cause for day and night, the reasons for eclipses. Then he discusses the origins of animal and vegetable life. His exposition deals with the origin of man, the ways of life of primitive folk, without fire or tillage or the arts of Lucretius' own relatively advanced civilization. Mankind, he thought, began to modify its savage ways as a result of family life and the mutual care of children. Nature taught men language. Out of gesture and speechlessness man evolved the habit of speech. Men learned to control fire out of the original gift of the lightning. Fire was not, as in the old Greek myth, the supernatural gift of a semidivine, though rebellious, Prometheus.

Lucretius' account of the rise of civilization is interesting. Kings founded cities and citadels as a refuge and stronghold for themselves. Gold was discovered and this destroyed honor; men will always follow the party of the rich. Then there came the rebellion of the poor and revolutions. And so magistrates were devised to temper the stubborn clash of rich and poor. Just as he denied that fire had been given to any semidivine Prometheus, so he believed it was not a goddess Athena who gave to men control of the various arts—of metalworking, of warfare and all its various techniques, weaving, agriculture with its various skills, music and the knowledge of the stars. It was the race of men, toiling endlessly, that created these advances in technique and civilization. And this, little by little, has advanced life to its high level and has stirred up from its depths the great tides

* W. E. Leonard and S. B. Smith, *T. Lucreti Cari de Rerum Natura* (Madison, 1942), p. 60.

of war. In his account of evolution, Lucretius ponders deeply the origin of religion and belief in the gods.

Lucretius and his school, the Epicureans, were pioneers in the development of the atomic theory. His position was quite simple. The whole universe could be explained in terms of atoms and space without postulating the intervention of the gods. Atoms, he thought, were falling endlessly in space, infinite space, combining, clinging together, forming infinitely rich and infinitely various combinations of things, to explain all the rich complexity and variety of the world as we know it. The whole material universe, the world of life and human activity, too, is in constant flux and change—some things coming into being and some passing away. But the sum of all things remains the same. The only reality is the changing world of matter. Even man's institutions and his thoughts are reflections of the changing material scene. The only changeless is the material substratum—the stuff from which the world and all that is in it is made. There is no ideal unity beyond the many. The unity of the world lies precisely in its materiality. Change is uniform and predictable and can, therefore, be reduced to law. There is no room in the world of Lucretius for surprising or supernatural occurrences, for miracle or divine caprice. "Nothing can come to be from nothing by divine decree." All change is slow change, everything proceeded by slow and imperceptible degrees; *nihil per saltum facit natura,* nature does nothing by leaps (through the poet, as opposed to the philosopher, does ample justice to the explosive moments in nature and history when, of a sudden, in the twinkling of an eye, the old is swept away, the new is born).

Two postulates were necessary for this school of thinkers in explaining the physical and social universe—atoms and space. Granted these two principles, they felt that everything in the world could be explained without bringing in the gods at all. The atoms (which he calls by many names) were solid, indestructible, and invisible. They are constantly in motion, begetting and destroying worlds and all that in them is. They are of many sizes and shapes; this accounts for differences of quality, texture, and shape in the world of things. Lightning will penetrate where fire will not, because it is composed of finer atoms. Light will pass through horn (the ancient equivalent of glass) on the side of a lantern when water will not; wine through a strainer when oil will not, for the same reason. Condiments and pickles tickle rather than wound our sense because their atoms are not smooth nor altogether hooked with jagged barbs, but slightly angled out. Hard substances are composed of hooked atoms; fluids of round smooth atoms which will not easily cohere (he uses a heap of poppy seed as an example). The sea is at once fluid and bitter. Its atoms must, therefore, be mixed—some smooth and round, but with painful rough ones mixed therein. This explains why it is possible to separate the salt from the water; why salt water can be purified and freshened if it filters through the ground.

The number of atom shapes was, he held, limited; the number of each shape, infinite. Although the texture, hardness, softness, etc., of things are dictated by atomic shapes, their color, odor, taste, and temperature are not. Worlds are infinite in number but finite in time. Our world is already in old age, has passed its creative prime.

In all this the reader may detect many crudities, many signs of inadequate theory or control of fact. He may be tempted to compare modern atomic theories to Lucretius' disadvantage. It would be more just, I think, to reflect how extraordinary is the insight; how exciting these analytical anticipations of the modern scientific world outlook, in spite of the inadequate scientific apparatus with which these men worked, in spite of their relatively primitive concepts of scientific method.

Lucretius was at one with the materialists of all ages in his concept of scientific method. He wanted his thinking to be understandable to the common man. He was careful to use simple, strong, plain, direct words and to use them in their natural meaning. He apologizes to his reader when he is forced to use a technical term from Greek philosophy for which there was no natural Latin equivalent. Logic chopping and the—to him—niggling arguments of his idealistic opponents he most heartily despised. When he contemplated the power of the senses to give knowledge to men he experienced a tremendous emotional uplift. All knowledge comes ultimately from sense experience. Reason cannot test or judge the senses because it owes its existence to them. One sense cannot correct another, sight, hearing, and so on. Nor can one sensation correct another, for they are all equally true.

Lucretius' opposition to religion is the key to his views on ethics, on the question how is it best for man to live. His answer to this question is twofold—positive and negative. On the negative side, Lucretius' answer is clear, articulate, resolute. Men must not live as most men now do, in a constant struggle for power and wealth. Avarice, ambition, lust, he thought, brought men no lasting happiness. No man has ever been more sensitively aware of the haunting dissatisfactions that dog mankind even in the midst of wealth and plenty and success. Most men do not know what they want for themselves. Man's greatness, well-being and happiness cannot be found in a multitude of possessions. He cannot find happiness or a well-nourished ego in wealth or success or pride of birth. Man's yearning for all these things is an expression of fear, of insecurity and consequent inner dissatisfaction. If only mankind could banish fear of insecurity! And here Lucretius makes a remarkable assumption. All these fears and agonies and strivings can be reduced to one fear—the fear of death. And the fear of death is poignant because men fear eternal torments after death. If then, Lucretius argues, we can banish once for all the fear of unending torments which men think await them when they die, then all fears will be done away and man can live in perfect peace, happiness, tranquillity. Here then is the reason, deep, urgent, compelling, for the study of philosophy. All human life is in question, not what one is to do in the next hour. To put his point of view briefly, bluntly, Lucretius believed that for the attainment of tranquillity of mind the most important single thing was the study of physics, a knowledge of the atomic philosophy. Out of this study would proceed the full emotional and intellectual realization of universal law, cause and effect, operative everywhere in the universe. Man would come to realize that nothing ever comes from nothing by divine decree but that all things are governed by order, regularity, consistency—in a word, by law. And so, he thought, fear would be banished, fear of the gods, of death, and of the torments after death. Thus mankind, embracing the "passionless bride, divine tranquillity," would come to lead a life that was altogether godlike. Was not that how the blessed gods themselves lived in the spaces between the stars? Not in a multitude of possessions, not in wealth, fame, eminence, or power could man find his inner satisfaction. Rather by renouncing all these things he might find peace. In passage after fervent passage our poet sings the praises of the simple life.

As an ethical thinker (at this particular stage of social and intellectual development) Lucretius was conscious of a paradox between his ethical teaching, which demanded freedom of the will for its realization, and his physics, which postulated the universal rule of law. This paradox he tried to solve, not too satisfactorily, by the doctrine of the swerve of the atoms. The atom swerve serves a twofold purpose in his system—it accounts for creation, for the passage from the homogeneous world of atoms to the heterogeneous world of things, and it accounts for freedom of the will by introducing an element of caprice into the very heart of things. In so brief an introduction to Lucretius' great poem there is no space for a discussion of this paradox. To many it has seemed a blemish on his system—notably to Cicero, who dismissed it as a puerile fiction. But whatever one's conclusion on this particular matter, there can be no doubt of Lucretius' general position in the history of thought. He has given us the most mature expression of philosophical materialism to come down to us from classical antiquity, and the most eloquent and poetical exposition of that creed of all time.

In this rendering of *De Rerum Natura,* mindful of Plato's admonition that the musical man in tuning a lyre does not try to outdo the musical man who has achieved perfection of pitch, I have not hesitated to borrow occasional phrases and even lines from Keats, Shelley, Gray, Tennyson, Cyril Bailey, and William Ellery Leonard where these seem to me to have attained perfection of rendering. No regular verse form can hope to reproduce the cadence of the Lucretian hexameter, and the attempt to use one can only result in distorting the thought by fitting it to the English meter. Prose, on the other hand, abandons any suggestion of the original poetic form without making possible the emphasis of verse. The translation of the *De Rerum Natura* has therefore been rendered in rhythmical lines of irregular length in order to adapt the verse to the ideas of the original rather than to expand or contract the thought of the poet to fit the verse scheme.

THE TEXT translated is that of BAILEY.

The

Roman Poet of Science

LUCRETIUS:

De Rerum Natura

Book One

Invocation to Venus

MOTHER OF AENEAS' CLAN, of man and gods delight,
Venus, all fostering, who under gliding stars in sky,
Dost make to teem ship-bearing sea, fruit-bearing earth;
Since every race of living things, through thee
Conceived, is born and sees the light of sun;
Thee, goddess, thee the winds do flee, and heaven's clouds,
Thee and thy advent;
For thee the chequered earth pours forth its lovely flowers,
For thee expanses of the sea do smile,
And tranquil sky does gleam when bathed in light.
When first the vernal face of day is seen,
The quickening breath of Zephyr is unlocked and strongly blows,
Then first the birds in air give word of thee,
Thee and thy coming,
Touched as they are in heart with power divine.
And then the beasts of field are driven wild,
To leap gay meadows and to swim swift streams.
And so a captive of thy charm, each thing in hot desire,
Will follow thee wherever thou dost go to lead him on.
Yes, and through seas and hills and headlong streams,
The leafy homes of birds and grassy fields
Putting sweet love in hearts of all,

3

Thou dost make them reproduce their race,
Kind after kind.

The poet prays to Venus for 'peace in our time'

SINCE thou alone are Nature's queen,
Without thy help can nothing come to shining shores of light,
Nothing is gay without thee, nothing loveable,
I want thy help in writing verse
The verse I try to write for Memmius, my friend.
(Hast thou not willed that he excel at every time, in every thing?)
So, goddess, give eternal beauty to my words;
Grant me that while I write
Fierce war on land and sea may sleep and rest.
For thou alone canst grant to mortal man
Peace and its blessings;
Since Mars, in arms all-powerful, rules the fierce works of war,
Thy lover, Mars, who often sinks upon thy breast
Completely overcome by love's eternal wound.
And so, in thy embrace,
His shapely head pillowed upon thy breast,
He gazes on thee, feeds his eager eyes with love,
His whole soul hangs upon thy lips.
Do thou, Divine, embracing him reclined, with holy frame,
Pour out sweet whispered words, O goddess famed,
And beg the quiet of peace for Roman folk.
I cannot carry out this task of mine with mind at peace
At such a crisis of my country's fate,
Nor could my Memmius betray his stock,
Or heedless be and fail his country's safety.
And so I pray for peace.
For all the gods enjoy eternal life in everlasting peace
Far, far away from all the troubles of our world.
Free from danger, free from grief, strong through their strength alone

The godhead needs us not,
Nor is it won by our deserts nor moved by wrath.

The poet begs his friend, Memmius, to be attentive

Now for the rest lend me attentive ears
And turn a piercing mind not burdened down with cares
To true philosophy.
I would not have these gifts of mine
Set out for you with constant, faithful zeal,
Disdained before they're understood.
For I propose to tell
The highest laws of heaven and the gods,
Reveal the primal stuff of things
And show how from this primaeval atom stuff
Creative nature forms all things, and grows and nurtures them;
To which again
This same creative nature breaks them up and sends them back.
And this in our account we call
Matter, creative stuff of things or seeds of things,
Or primal bodies, some might say,
Because from these as elementary principles
Emerge all things that are.

How his teacher, Epicurus, was the first to defy 'religions and the threats of priests'

WHEN human life lay foully prone upon the ground
Conspicuous to see,
Crushed by creed and myth, like ponderous weights,
Which like incarnate horror from the skies looked down
And lowered over man with visage grim,
A man of Greece first dared to raise his mortal eyes against
And even stand and fight.
And him no fables told of gods could daunt,

5

Nor heaven with lightning flash or thunderbolt dismay.
But only stirred the more the valorous splendor of his mind.
He longed to be the first to crack the cramping bonds of nature.
And so his splendid strength of soul prevailed.
Outside he went, beyond the flaming ramparts of the world
And ranged the infinite whole in mind and thought's imagining.
And from his mental voyages to us brought back,
Like conqueror crowned in victory, the news of Nature's laws
Of what could come to be and what could not,
The code that binds each thing, its deep-set boundary stone.
And so religion in its turn is trampled under foot and trodden down,
And man is made like god by one man's victory.

The evil deeds of religion is exemplified by the sacrifice of Iphigeneia

ONE fear I have in this long argument,
That even Memmius might think
We're impiously dabbling in profane philosophy
And setting wanton foot on sin's broad way.
Rather religion has itself begot
Impious and bloody deeds.
Think how at Aulis, Grecian chiefs, picked leaders of mankind
Stained altars of the chaste and huntress queen
With maiden's blood in obscene rite and wanton sacrifice.*
And she, poor girl, the fillets on her maiden locks,
Adorning either cheek,
Saw father stand by sacral stone, stedfast but sombre;
The slaves of sacrifice with swords concealed

* This is Lucretius' account of a well known legend, the sacrifice of Iphigeneia by her father, Agamemnon. When the Greek fleet was delayed by contrary winds at Aulis, the soothsayer Calchas announced that the goddess Artemis had been offended, and could only be propitiated by the sacrifice of the child of one of the leaders. Agamemnon summoned his daughter Iphigeneia, under pretence of marrying her to Achilles, and offered her up.

To spare a father's natural sympathy,†
The clansfolk weeping at the doleful spectacle;
In tongueless terror down she fell and swooned.
Poor girl, it could not help at all at such a time
That she had long ere this been first to call him father.
For borne aloft in rough men's hands, poor trembling girl,
Not tenderly like bride in husband's grasp
(To altar led the escort not to wedlock's home),
No wedding hymn, but funeral chant, accompanied her
Who chastely died by wanton act
Just when love's consummation should be hers.
And so she died,
A sad and sacrificial victim at a father's blow,
That jealous god by butchery propitiate
Might grant auspicious voyage to the fleet.
That is religion, these its monstrous acts.

*In order to banish the fear of death, men must answer fundamental
questions about the soul*

MEMMIUS, you too will want to fall away from me
Even you,
Quite vanquished by the fear-provoking words of priests.
How many things can priests invent,
Vain myths to sap a lifetime's reasoning
And muddy fortune's every gift with fear.
No wonder; for if men could see
There is to misery a fixed ordainéd end,
In some way they'd find strength
To stand against religion and the threats of priests.

† Scholars have usually given the words *propter hunc* a purely locative force—near
him. I think these scholars miss a characteristic piece of Lucretius' ironic savagery. The
slaves conceal their swords on his account, in deference to his feelings. I render it 'to
spare a father's natural sympathy.'

But as it is no principle is there
No chance to rally and stand fast,
Since fear of endless torments makes us shrink from death.
For men are ignorant about the soul.
Was it like body born?
Or did it make its way into our bodies when these came to birth?
Will soul die too, by death asunder torn
Or will it live to see the shades of Hell, Hell's mighty swamps?
Or will soul make its way
Into the mortal frame of other creatures by divine decree?
As our own Ennius believed, our Roman Ennius,
Who was the first to pluck from lovely Helicon a wreath,
Green and immortal in its foliage,
To sing the deeds of men among the folk of Italy.
Yet Ennius assuredly maintained in his immortal verse
That Hell there was;
But did not think
Bodies or souls of men could linger there
But only wraiths and copies wondrous pale.
Homer, he thought, came up from Acheron
Homer the peerless, poet unsurpassed,
Came up from lower depths, wept salty tears
And told him tales about the shape of things.
And so we must be clear about the laws of things above
About the laws that govern sun and moon
About the force that moves all things on earth.
This above all we have to comprehend with piercing mind,
The soul and mind of what stuff they are made.
And visions too that haunt our waking eyes
Much more when we're diseased or lulled in sleep
So that we seem to see our dead friends face to face,
Hold converse with them
Though we know full well they're really dead,

8

Their bones the earth enfolds.
I know how difficult my topic is
How hard to illustrate in Latin verse
Profound inventions of the thoughtful Greeks.
Our mother tongue is ill-equipped with words for topics new.
But still the wondrous worth of you,
The joy I hope to gain from your sweet friendship
Makes me want to bear all toil,
Labor the still nights through,
In search of language and in search of song,
To bring illumination to your mind,
To help you see the heart of hidden, murky things.
And so this darkened terror of the mind must be dispelled,
Not by the rays of sun or gleaming shafts of day,
But Nature's laws, by looking in her face.

No thing can come from nothing by divine decree

Our first beginning must set out from this;
No thing can come from nothing by divine decree.
For, you see,
Fear so possesses every mortal heart
Because so many things are seen to happen on earth and in the sky,
For which men find no cause.
They think these happen by divine decree.
Wherefore when we have seen
That nothing comes to be from nothing,
Then more clearly we shall see the object of our search,
Whence each thing can be created and how can come to be,
Without the help of gods.
For if everything came to be from nothing
Every species could be random born,
There'ld be no need of seeds.
Men could arise from sea,

9

The scaly race of fish from earth,
Birds could explode from sky.
And beasts both wild and tame by random birth could roam
Ploughland and wilderness alike.
And fruits on trees would never stay the same,
But change.
All creatures could produce all offspring.
If all things did not have their procreant seeds
How could they have a fixed and changeless mother?
But as it is
Because each thing is made from certain seeds
From these the thing is born and comes to shores of light,
When stuff appropriate to each
And proper elements are there;
All things cannot come from everything,
Because in everything there is a separate hidden power.
Again in spring we see the rose,
In summer corn; the grapes at autumn's prompting.
Why? But that seeds of things together come;
When time is ripe the fashioned thing appears,
When season's right and teeming earth brings forth
The tiny fragile things in safety to the shores of light?
But if they came to be from nothing,
They would suddenly explode to birth
At random times and inappropriate seasons of the year,
Because, you see, there'ld be no elements
To keep them from cohering and from birth
Till time is ripe.
Nor need there'ld be for space of time for things to grow
If they could grow from nothing.
Babies would suddenly be men
And shrubs would swift and sudden leap from earth.
But nothing now like this occurs,

Since all things slowly grow from proper matter,
As is right,
And as they grow retain their natural kind.
So you may know that all things wax
From atom stuff appropriate.
This too is true;
Without the showers at proper season of the year,
Earth could not produce her gay and teaming brood.
Nor without food could nature nurture living things in kind
Nor save their life.
So you must rather think
That in the multiplicity of things are common elements,
Like alphabet in words,
Than that a thing can come to be without its atom stuff appropriate.
Then, why could not nature fashion men so huge
That they could pass on foot through ocean's depths
Or with their strength of arm tear hills apart?
Or men whose length of life could far surpass
A man's allotted span?
Surely because there is atomic stuff assigned to each,
Determining what can come to be.
And so confess we must
That nothing ever comes to be from nothing,
Since things need 'seeds',
That each created thing can be produced
And brought to air's soft breezes.
Last argument;
We see that well-worked fields surpass a wilderness
That man by toil of hands can bring forth better crops.
Therefore, atomic particles must lurk in earth,
Which we by turning fertile glebe, subduing sod,
Can bring to birth.

If there were not, we'd see all things improve
Without the agency of human toil, spontaneously.

Nothing is ever brought to nothingness

AND now another thought is yours to grasp;
Nature resolves all things to atom forms
That nothing wholly dies.
For if, through all its parts a thing
Were subject to destruction
Suddenly t'would die and vanish from our sight.
There'ld be no need of outer force to break it up,
Dissolve its joints.
But now because a thing is made
Compacted of eternal seeds,
Till it encounter force to break it up, to smash it at a blow,
Or penetrate its joints, encompass dissolution,
Nature does not permit that death of anything be seen.
Again when time removes a thing from mortal sight
And wastes it by decay,
If all its atom stuff should perish too,
How could the queen of love bring plants and animals
Kind after kind to birth again,
Restore them to the shores of light?
How could chequered, creative earth once they were born,
Give food to nurse and nurture them
Kind after kind?
How could the native springs and rivers flowing from without
Keep the sea full?
And how could aether feed the stars?
For endless age, the span of time's infinity,
Would have destroyed
All things from mortal body made.
But if through all the endless past the atoms have endured

From which the sum of things is made, is ever made anew,
Then surely the atomic sum is blest with immortality.
And so it cannot be
That all things should be brought to naught.
Again,
The self-same force, the self-same cause,
Would smash all things alike,
Unless eternal matter held them bound
With lashings close or loose.
A touch would be sufficient cause for death
Were there not atoms with eternal life;
To break up these a special mighty force appropriate would be re-
quired.

But as things are because the atom stuff
Though variously joined and woven into things,
Endures forever,
So it comes about
That things endure as well,
Until a force is found powerful enough to smash and overcome
Texture of each.
So can nothing ever back to nothingness return.
All things are sucked at death
Back to the stream of matter,
And in the eternal storage house of matter stored.
Just so the showers of rain all die,
When father sky has hurled them in the womb of mother earth.
But shining crops spring up,
The boughs on trees grow green
The trees themselves increase and bear their clustered fruit.
And so the race of men and beasts is fed, finds nourishment;
And so we see our cities teem with young,
The leafy woods alive with song of birds;
And flocks wearied with weight of fat,

Lie down in fruitful fields.
And so the rich white stream of milk
Pours from distended udders.
And so the new young brood of tiny lambs
Sports wantonly in fresh green fields
With tiny tottering limbs,
The while their infant hearts
Thrill at fresh milk.
And so we see
That all things do not perish utterly.
Nature creates the new from out the old,
And lets no thing be born without another's death.

Atoms are invisible but so are many other bodies
Examples: Wind, smell, heat, cold, sound. Clothes that grow damp
or dry. The ring on your finger, the statue worn by the passer-by,
the pavements of the streets

Now come, since I have taught that things
Cannot be made from nothingness
Nor once they're born can back to nothingness be called,
Lest you should find it hard to credit these my words
Because your eyes have never seen and cannot see atomic stuff,
Let me recall to you some things you've never seen
Yet which, you must admit, exist, are real.
First then the strong awakened force of wind
Lashes the sea, destroys great ships and scatters clouds
Or sometimes tears o'er plains in headlong course,
Tears up great trees and leaves them strown;
Or smites the topmost hills with blasts that rend the woods.
With mighty din the oceans rage in tempests angry roar.
And so we must be sure
There is an unseen force of wind
That, in its headlong course, sweeps sea and land

Yes, and the heaven's clouds;
And all things this same wind will tear and rend
In sudden onslaught of the hurricane.
The wind spreads havoc in its headlong course
Just like the rush of water.
Water itself is soft;
But when a sudden shower sweeps from the hills after a fall of rain
With force torrential it can sweep along
The broken fragments from the woods;
Yes, and whole trees.
The strongest bridge must yield before the force of sweeping flood.
The river too, muddy from copious rain,
Dashes against the mighty driven piles.
With sickening roar it spreads destruction round,
Rolls mighty rocks along and everything that bars its path.
Just so the blasts of wind are onward borne like mighty streams
And when they strike a thing,
Roll it around and push it on
With constant blows.
Or pick it up in eddying whirl,
Take it away in swirling hurricane.
And so maintain I must,
The wind's a mighty force invisible,
In deeds and action rivalling headlong streams.
Yet streams are visible.
And then again,
We know the various scents of things,
Yet nothing can we see that meets the nose.
And heat and cold our eyes can never see,
Nor onset of the voice.
And yet these things we know are bodily,
Because they smite the sense.
Nothing can touch, be touched, unless it's bodily.

Often are clothes hung up on shore to dry
Where ocean breaks its waves.
Here they grow damp but in the sun grow dry.
Yet human eyes have never seen the moisture coming in,
Nor yet again depart.
The particles of damp are small—
Too small for eyes to see.
Again as rolling sun brings back the rolling years
The ring you wear on finger grows more thin;
The steady drip of water wears a stone;
The curving iron of plowshares in the unmarked lapse of time
Grows smaller in the fields.
The paving stones in streets are worn by feet of multitudes.
Bronze statues by the gateways show their right hands worn,
Worn ever by the passer-by who greets them and departs.
We see these things grow smaller, wear away.
And yet the particles that leave as fleeting moments pass
We never see.
The parsimonious nature of our sight forbids.
Lastly when time and nature makes things slowly grow,
Makes them develop bit by bit
These small additions straining eyes can never see.
When things grow old from time and slow decay,
When rocks above the sea are ground to sand
Worn by the silent gnawing of the sea's salt spray,
What momently they lose you never see.
And so by means of bodies small and imperceptible,
Nature must work her will.

There is space or void in things

AND yet
The nature of matter cannot keep all things
Close packed.

There must be space, or, void, in things.
To know of this you'll find a useful thing in many ways.
For knowing this you'll not go wandering in doubt
Nor speculate about the sum of things
Nor doubt my words.
And so there is a void,
Space empty, space untouchable.
If there were not, by no means could things move.
For that which is matter's one peculiar task,
To block and hinder—would affect all things at all times.
Nothing could move.
Nothing could find the principle of moving space.
But as it is,
Through seas and lands and heaven's heights,
So many things we see, moving so many ways,
In fashions various before our eyes.
But if there were no void,
We'd have to think them always still,
Always deprived of restless, anxious motion.
Or rather never could they e'er have come to be
In any way at all.
Their stuff on all sides would have lain
In close packed stillness.
Even when things seem solid to your eyes,
From this you'll learn they're really made of rarer stuff.
In rocks and caves the water trickles through
And all things seem to weep with copious drops.
And food can creep through pores of every living thing,
Bushes will grow and bring forth fruit in time.
Because the nourishment can make its way,
Through stems and boughs.
Voices can go through walls and pass closed doors of homes.
The stiffening cold can reach our marrow bones.

Were there not space through which these things might pass,
This could not be.
And why could thing surpass a thing in weight,
Though like in size?
If equal matter were in ball of wool or lead
Its weight should be the same,
Since body's task it is to push all objects down.
So when a thing is just as big but lighter weighs than other thing
From this we know there's more of space in it.
The lighter thing of equal weight avows
Less matter lurks in it.
And so there's something mixed in things
That eager mind can grasp—
That which we call the void, or empty space.
Now I'll discuss a point which some allege
Lest you be drawn away from truth.
They say that waters open up a way when fishes swim
And leave a liquid path.
And this they say because the fishes leave behind a place
To which the waters flow again when fishes leave.
And so they argue other things can move and change their place
Although the whole is firm and full.
The reasoning is false, the concept wrong.
How could the fish advance
Unless the waters left a space?
Where can the waters go that fish cannot?
And so confess we must
That were it not for void in things
That everything would stand and never change,
Not knowing change or variableness.
Or else confess there is a void in things
Whence every individual thing
Can find its start of motion.

18

And then, if two broad bodies swiftly leap apart
After they meet,
Surely the cause must be
That air possesses all the void that lies between.
It matters not how fast the air comes in, in whirling stream,
The empty space between is not entirely filled
In just one instant.
The air must fill the spaces one by one
And then possess the whole.
If any think when bodies leap apart
That this results from condensation in the atmosphere
Clearly he's wrong.
If this were true
That would be empty which was full before
That which was empty, full.
Air cannot condense in such a way.
Nor if it could, as I maintain
Could air without the void,
Withdraw into itself and summon to one place
Its several parts.
And so although reluctant to admit the truth
(You've long held back)
Still now you must confess there is a void in things.
Now many things I still could tell
To build up high conviction for my words.
But for a keen and subtle mind few traces are enough.
The rest you can detect yourself.
For hunting dogs can often find by scent
The lair of mountain ranging beasts
Though hid in leaves.
So you, in themes like this, can follow track,
Trace out the truth by scenting step on step,
Find out the secret lairs where truth is hid.

But if you fail or swerve a little from the track,
This promise plain, I'll make you, Memmius:
Such copious draughts as from a mighty fountain deep
Will my sweet tongue pour out from teeming breast,
Before the flood of argument in verse assailed your ears
Before my verse had compassed just one theme,
I fear old age would creep upon your limbs,
And death would loosen all the joints of life.

> *Everything in the universe is made of atoms and space. There cannot be a third principle*

BUT now again to weave my task in words,
The whole of Nature is of two things built,
Atoms and void.
The void in which the atom forms are placed
In which they move, hither and yon.
The universal sense of eyes and ears declare to men
Bodies exist.
Unless our faith in sense is grounded sure and strong,
Beyond the sense there's not a single principle
To which we can appeal to prove a thought about the hidden things
By reason's sheer unaided power,
Nothing could prove by reasoning of the mind.
Were there not room and empty space
The space which we call void
No bodies ever, anywhere could find a place
Nor could they move at all in various ways.
And this I've proved to you a little while ago.
Besides these two first principles,
There could not be a third constituent in the eternal scheme of things
Severed alike from body and from void.
For whatsoever is, must, of necessity,
Be something in itself.

And if it can be touched, however small and light the touch
It swells the sum of things by increase small or great,
Provided only that it *is* at all.
If it's beyond the reach of touch
It has no power to stop another thing from passing through,
Right through itself and passing on its way.
It then must be what we've described
As empty space or void.
Again whate'er exists
Must either act on things, be acted on,
Or else allow action, reaction somewhere in its frame.
Unless it's bodily, no thing can act, be acted on, or space afford
For action and reaction; unless it's empty space or void.
And so apart from void and bodies there can never be
A third constituent in the scheme of things.
Nothing to move our sense at any time
Or let itself be grasped by reasoning of the mind.

A digression on substance and accidents

AND now you'll find essential qualities
Linked to everything that can have a name
Or accidental qualities.
The first we'll thus define;
A property that can at no time, anywhere,
Be taken from a thing
Without destroying it, in its essential self.
Of such is weight for rocks and heat to fire
To water, moisture and to every body, touch;
But touchlessness to void.
The second these will illustrate;
Riches or poverty, freedom, slavery or war or peace,
Can come and go but still the thing itself abides untouched.
And so we rightly call these accidents.

And likewise time cannot exist itself,
But from the flight of things we get a sense of time.
This thing was finished in the past while this goes on,
And this will be hereafter.
No man, we must confess, feels time itself,
But only knows of time from flight or rest of things.
Again when people say that Tyndarus' daughter has been carried off,
Or Trojan tribes were overcome in war,
And say these tales are true, exist,
Beware we must, lest they compel us to avow
That these events are real,
Because the past has carried off these men beyond recall;
When for these men the events themselves
Were philosophical accidents.
For what occurred was really accident,
Either for these lands themselves,
Or else the realms of space.
Again, if substance had not been
Nor place nor space in which each thing was carried on
Never would passion's flame, kindled in Trojan heart,
By beauty of the Grecian maid,
Have kindled blazing fires of savage war,
Nor would the wooden horse have tricked the Trojan hosts,
Set Troy aflame with midnight birth of Greeks.
So you may see that all events from first to last
Are not like body, cannot exist themselves and by themselves,
Nor be described as void.
It's right to call them accidents of body and of space,—
The space where things go on.
Bodies are sometimes elements of things
And sometimes objects made from union of the elements
The elements themselves no force can ever quench.
Their solid force must be in the end prevail.

I know it's hard to think that anywhere in things
Are bodies found and elements with solid frames.
The thunderbolt can penetrate through the solid walls of a house,
Just as do shouts and cries.
And iron grows white in fire and rocks break up
Smashed by the fiery force of heat.
And hard gold melts and softens in the flames,
The ice of brass dissolves.
Both heat and cold can come through silver cups.
We know, we've held the goblet in our hands
And felt them both alike
When slaves poured in the liquid from above.
And so there seems to be in things
No hard solidity.
But just because exactitude of thought, and nature, too,
Both hem us in, pause and attend.
In verses few I will expound the truth;
That elements there are of body, very hard,
These are eternal and that from these
The sum of things which now we've come to know
Was made.
And so our doctrine is
That these are elements and seeds of things.
Come now, since we have found
A double nature of two different things
Body and space—in which all things go on,
Follow it must that each of these exist itself,
Alone unmixed.
Wherever space lies empty this we call the void.
Where body stands, that's never empty space.
And so atomic elements must solid be
And free from space.
Now since in things created

Void or space exits,
Follow it must that solid stuff stands round enclosing space.
Nor could accuracy of thought allow
That anything holds space within itself
Unless you grant it's solid matter that the space enfolds.
And that which keeps the space in things could nothing be
Except a union of material things.
Matter itself then,
Because of solid body made
Can endless be
When all else is dissolved.
Were there not void, the whole would solid be.
Were there not bodies fixed to fill the space they hold
The universe would nothing be but empty space.
And so assuredly we see
That body's quite distinct from void and turn about,
Nor void to body like.
Since th' universe is not entirely full,
Nor empty quite.
And so there are established forms of things
To mark off empty space from what is full.
These forms or atoms cannot be dissolved
By blows delivered from outside,
And no internal force can reach their heart and break them up;
In no way can they dissolution find.
All this I've shown you just a little while before.
For clear it is,
That nothing could be crushed without the void,
Or smashed or cut in two.
Nor could it take in moisture to itself,
Or spreading cold or piercing fire,
Which brings most things to end.
The more a thing possesses void within,

The more by all these forces it is inwardly assailed,
Begins to break.
And so the atoms solid, free from void,
Must everlasting be.
And if the primal stuff of things,
Were not endued with power to last for evermore,
Long while ago the things we see,
Would all have passed away, would all have come to nothingness,
From nothingness had all we see been born.
And since I've shown above
That nothing ever can from nothing come,
Nor what's once made, to nothingness return,
The atoms must eternal be;
To atoms at the last must all things be resolved,
Providing matter for the things to come.
And so the atoms are of solid singleness
Preserved through time from endless time
To make all things anew.

Division can not go on indefinitely

AGAIN if Nature had no limit placed to breaking things
By now material bodies would be brought so low
By Time's destructive force in ages past,
That nothing out of them could be conceived
Within fixed Time
And reach the final span of life.
For anything you name
Is quicker broken up than it could be renewed.
And so what endless age of Time's infinity
Had broken up and smashed
Could never be renewed in all the time to come.
But as it is, assuredly,
Because a limit is to breaking up of things assigned

We see all kinds of things renewed
We see a settled time assigned to things,
Kind after kind,
In which they can attain the flower of life.

The atomic theory enables us to explain softer things

THIS further fact will help us win belief:
Though atom forms are made of solid stuff
We still can give account of softer things—
Of earth and water, air and fire,
Of what force each is made, by what power goes its way,
When once we know that void is mixed in things.
But, if we thought the atoms soft,
Then reason's power could never make it plain
How hard things came to be—like flint or iron,
For nature would entirely lack a principle on which to found itself.
And so confess we must that atom bodies are—
Splendid in solid singleness,
And these when joined and linked in unity,
Things too are riveted in unity,
To show their sturdy strength.
But were no limit set to breaking up of things,
Still we must assume that things of every kind survive,
Right to this day through endless lapse of time
Of such a kind that never yet were they assailed,
By any danger.
But since their nature's frail,
It makes no sense
That they endure through endless time,
By countless blows assailed.
Now since to all things kind by kind is limit set
Of growth, maintaining life,

And since by Nature's laws is set for each a principle,
What it can do and what cannot,
So that it changes not,
So that all things stand fast,
That various birds in due array
Display their species with their bodies' marks,
They must assuredly possess a frame,
Of stuff unchangeable.
For could the atoms be subdued and change,
Then Nature's laws would also be subdued
The laws of what can come to be and what cannot,
The power that binds each thing, its deep set boundary stone.
Nor could the race of beasts and birds and men,
Kind after kind,
Reflect their parent's ways,
Their manners, customs, even gait.
Now more in atoms which our sense can never grasp,
There is a series of irreducible points,
Of which each point, we may be sure,
Is indivisible and very small.
It never has existed by itself nor will it ever come to be alone,
Since every atom form exists
A primary and single part
Of some thing else.
And other atom parts and others yet in close array,
Make up the nature of the thing.
Since by themselves they cannot stand alone,
They needs must cling to other atom forms,
And from this unity cannot be torn.
And so the atoms are of solid singleness,
A close dense mass of tiny parts
Not put together by a union of the parts

27

But rather always strong in solid singleness.
From these atomic forms,
Nature, keeping safe the seeds of things,
Will not allow that anything should be removed or torn away.
Unless there were these atoms, infinitely small,
Then smallest things would be composed
Of countless parts.
For half of half will always have a half,
And so on to infinity.
And then what difference would there be,
Between the least and greatest thing?
Why none at all.
For though the sum of things were infinite,
Yet smallest things would yet have parts,
In number infinite.
But this the reason never could accept
And will not let the mind believe.
At last you must submit, confess
That tiny things there are of nature indivisible.
Since this is so, this, too, you must allow,
That these atomic shapes are made of solid stuff,
And will for evermore endure.
Again if Nature, creative queen of everything,
Decreed that all things must be broken up
Into their finest parts,
Then none of them she could create again,
Because a thing that's not increased by any parts,
Lacks all the powers which stuff creative must possess,
Coherence in its various forms,
The power to meet and parry weights and blows,
The power to move, the powers in short,
By which all things in this our universe are carried on.

The poet refutes those who like Heraclitus think that fire is the first constituent of things

Now some have thought
That fire is basic to the sum of things,
The universe composed of fire alone.
But men who think like this have wandered very far from truth.
And Heraclitus was the chief of these, the first to join the fray,
Renowned he was for sayings dark,
But more admired by fools,
Than sober, thoughtful Greeks who sought the truth.
For men of stolid wits are wont to love the more, admire the more,
The things they see,
Lurking in twisted words.
Dull oafs like this set up for truth
What sweetly tickles human ears,
What's most tricked out in pretty sound.
I hasten to enquire,
Whence the variety in things
If all are made from simple fire unmixed?
Nor could it help at all
That fire condense in turn and then again grow rare,
If all the parts of fire
Had nature like fire's total sum.
For when its parts together drew,
Then fiercer would fire flame.
If parts again were scattered wide
The flame grows weak.
From such a cause there's nothing you could think of that could come
                                                            to be,
Far less the rich diversity of things—from fire condensed or rare.
This too is true;
If only they'd confess that void is mixed in things

Then easily they'd prove that fires condense, grow rare.
But since this teacher's book,
Though full of inspiration manifest,
Leaves many contradictions in his path,
And makes his pupils shrink from leaving void unmixed in things,
Dreading the heights they lose the track of truth;
They fail to see—with void removed from things,
All things condensed would form one entity,
Not many things.
And this one entity in its hot course,
Could not emit a substance from itself.
And so,
Because the warming fire sends out both light and heat,
From this you see its parts are not close packed.
But if you think in other ways
Fire may be quenched and change its form
And grudge not to allow a thing like this at any point,
Then we may be sure,
All heat will come to nothing utterly,
And all created things from nothing come.
For whatsoever is changed, beyond its limit goes,
This straightway is the death of that which went before.
For something in these fires must needs survive,
Be left unharmed,
Or else all things to nothing utterly return,
The store of things be born again, grow strong,
From nothing.
But since there are fixed atom forms which ever keep their shape
And as these come and go and change arrangement,
Things change their shape, bodies are altered too,
You can be sure
That these atomic particles
Are never fire.

Nor could it mean a thing,
That certain parts can leave and some remain,
That others were assigned,
That order, placed, arrangement change,
If all things kept the form of fire.
The things
That took created form from particles of fire,
Would still in every way be fire.
This is the truth I think;
It is the atom forms
Whose meeting, movement, order and position; yes and shape
Make fire.
When the positions of the atom forms are changed
The nature of the 'thing' resulting changes too.
These atom particles are not like fire or any other thing
Which sends off bodies to our consciousness
And by their contact move our sense of touch.
To say that fire is everything,
That nothing else is real in all the sum of things
As this same early thinker does,
Seems like a madman's babbling.
He starts with sense,
And yet he fights against the sense,
Weakens the evidence of that on which he thinks
All things must hang.
For not grasp every other thing that's just as bright to see.
This seems to me both vain and mad.
For where's a court to which to make appeal?
What firmer test of truth can mankind find than sense
To mark off true and false?
Then why should any one annul all other things
And posit fire alone?
Rather than hold that fire does not exist

And posit other substances?
To hold to either creed seems just as mad.

Those who posit earth or air or moisture are just as wrong

So those who thought that fire's the substance of the universe,
From fire the sum of things was made,
And those who think that air performs this role,
Or those who think that moisture alone has fashioned everything,
Or those who think that earth created everything
And took the form of all created things
All these have wandered very far from truth.
And those who posit two first principles
Add air to fire, to moisture earth,
I blame them equally.

Even Empedocles went wrong in positing four first principles

And also those who think from four first principles
Have all things come—
From earth and air, from moisture and fire
They're just as wrong.
Of these the chief, Empedocles of Acragas,
Was born in Sicily.
That island with its triple coast, surrounded by the Ionian sea,
With many a winding cove,
Where great, green breakers splash in salty foam,
While in its narrow straits the tearing sea,
Shuts off the island from the land of Italy.
And here is dread Charybdis, famed in song,
And here the rumblings deep of Aetna's mighty mount,
That seems to gather once again the flames of wrath,
To belch again the bursting fires from savage throat
And send its flashing flames to reach the sky.

And though this island seems in many ways
A wondrous place to human eyes, worthy to see,
Rich with good things and great with power of men,
Yet nothing has it ever held that's comparable with this great man,
Nothing more holy, nothing more wonderful, more dear.
The words of his inspired and godlike heart
Have raised their voice, expounded all his great discoveries,
That scarcely does he seem to be of human stock.
Yet he and others whom I've named before,
Lesser than he by far and far beneath,
Yet these have thought of many things in good and godlike way,
And uttered from their hearts as from a shrine,
Words far more wise, with reason far more sure,
Than ever Pythian priestess from the laurelled shrine
And tripod of the Delphic god.
And yet they often went astray in their first principles.
Great were these men, great and calamitous their fall.
First they neglected void, yet thought that things could move;
Allowed things rare and soft—the air, the sun, the rain,
The earth and beasts and crops,
But leave no empty space in all of these.
And secondly,
No end they saw to process of dividing things,
No limit to their breaking up, nor ever, anywhere a least.
And yet we see there is a furthest point in everything
Presented to our senses as the least.
From this you can infer
The furthest point invisible is least of all.
And more since they suppose
The elementary form of things is soft
The fundamental substance made of stuff
We know can come to birth, we know endowed with mortal frame,
This follows then, that all things must to nothing utterly return;

And then, the store of things be born again, grow strong,
From nothing.
How far from truth they stray you know by now.
Then too these theories are mutually opposed,
And poison to each other.
So when they meet assuredly they'll die, or fly apart,
As now you see in thunder storms the thunder bolts and rain and

                                            winds

Fly quickly far apart.
Again,
If all created things are held to come from four first principles
To these again are held to be resolved,
How can these four be called first principles of things
Rather than things of them?
For they're created turn by turn, their colours change
And all their nature, too, from endless time.
But if you think corporeal forms of fire
And earth and breeze and moisture so unite
That in this union none of them are changed,
Then you will see that nothing could be made from them,
No living thing, no lifeless body—like a tree.
Rather in such a union of things unlike
Each will reveal itself, show its true self.
Air will be seen as mixed with earth; moisture with heat.
But in begetting things
The elements should bring to bear a secret unseen form
That nothing might stand out or fight against the union,
Or stop created thing from achieving its new form.
But as it is you see
They trace it back to sky and fires of sky
Assume that fire can turn itself into the winds of sky,
That thence comes rain, and earth can come from rain.
And then again the process in reverse—

That from the earth can come,
First moisture, then the air, and then the heat.
But elemental principles should not behave like this.
There must be something that abides unchangeable
In order that the sum of things should not be brought to nothingness.
For whatsoe'er is changed, beyond its limit goes
This straightway is the death of that which went before.
Now since the things we've named above are subject to exchange
It's clear they must be made from other things
Which cannot change or alteration find,
Or else you'd find all things return to nothingness.
Were it not better to assume atomic forms?
And if from these by chance the fire were made,
Adding a few and taking some away,
Their movement and their order changed
Then air results.
And so with this hypothesis
All things can change themselves to other things
Because all come from atoms.
But Memmius, you may argue thus;
'The patent facts of things reveal
That all things grow, are nurtured from the earth,
And rise to meet the breezes;
Unless when time of year is right the rain abounds,
That shrubs and trees are pelted with the stress of storm,
Unless the sun will warm and cherish them,
Then crops and trees and animals alike,
Could never grow.'
Yes and it's true,
Unless dry food, soft moisture, too, assisted human kind,
We, too, should die, would lose our flesh,
And all the life be loosened from our sinews and our bones.
Assuredly we're nourished and we're nurtured by fixed elements.

All other species, too, kind after kind.
Of this we may be sure
It's just because atomic elements
Common so many ways to many things
Are mixed in things,
That all the various species all are fed on divers foods.
And often it's a matter of profound significance
With just what atoms other atoms join,
And how they're placed, arranged,
What motions they receive, transmit among themselves;
Because, you see,
From these atomic shapes are built so many things,
Sky and the sea and earth,
Rivers and sun and crops and trees and living things,
In various movements, various mixtures linked.
It's just the same in all these verses that you read.
Scattered throughout the whole are letters—in number infinite,
And yet you have to grant that words and verse alike
Will differ widely both in sense and power of sound.
Majestic is the power of letters when their order's changed.
But atoms bring to bear wider variety,
And so create,
A rich and infinitely wide diversity of things.

Anaxagoras, too, went astray

Now let us search the famous theory of a famous man,
Homoeomeria of Anaxagoras.
My native tongue's too poor in scientific terms
To let me name it in the Latin speech.
And yet the thought itself is easy to expound.
First what he calls the *homoeomeria* of things.
You see he thought that bones were made
Of very small and tiny bones,

And flesh likewise of small and tiny bits of flesh;
That blood is made when many drops of blood together come;
And gold again from tiny grains of gold,
And earth from fragments made from little earths;
And likewise fire from fire, water from water;
All the rest he pictures and imagines the same way.
Yet this mighty thinker will not grant
That there is void in any part of nature's whole,
Nor limit to the cutting up of things.
In both these points he seems to me to go astray,
Just as those others did.
Another fault it seems to me in him is this—
First principles in his imagining are much too weak
(If you could call those things first principles,
Which have a nature like the things they form,
Suffer like them, like them are doomed to pass away,
And nothing holds them from the doom of nothingness).
For which of all his principles,
Is able to endure in face of pressures ultimate,
Escape from death when ground between the jaws
Of final devastation?
Fire, you suppose? Moisture or air? Or bones or blood?
Not one of these I think.
For all of them will die
As much as things we see before our eyes
And pass away, by violence trampled down and overcome.
As witness here I call what I've proved long before.
Nothing can pass away to nothingness,
Nor yet from nothingness can one thing grow.
And now since food it is that nourishes and rears
Our frame corporeal,
From this you know that veins and blood and bones

Yes and our sinews, too, all these are made from parts of heterogeneous kind.

Or if they hold that all that nurtures us,
Our food, I mean, is made of mingled elements,
In them resides small bits of sinew, bones and veins and blood,
Then they must hold that all our food—liquid or dry alike
Is made from parts of heterogeneous kind—
Of bones and sinews, ichor and blood together mixed.
And then if all the things that grow from earth
Are there potentially in particles of earth,
The earth must be composed of things,
Heterogeneous in kind that rise from earth.
And try this in another field.
The self same words you'll use again.
Suppose in logs that flame should lurk,
And smoke and ash,
Why logs are then composed of things
Heterogeneous in kind, of heterogeneous things which rise from logs.
Of all the things which earth can nurture and can rear
The same is true.

.   .   .   .   .   .

And here's a tiny chance to hide
Which Anaxagoras grasps.
He thinks that all things mingled lurk in things,
But one stands out—
The one the compound holds the more in quantity,
That's stationed more in front and so stands out.
In this, of course, he's very far from truth.
For were he right then this we'd see.
When corn were crushed by threatening strength of rock,
Some sign of blood,
Or of the things that in our body lurk, are nurtured there.
Then when we grind the corn, and rub it stone on stone,

38

Blood should ooze out.
And blades of grass and pools of water, too,
Should ooze sweet drops, in savor like the milk of fleecy beasts.
And when the clods of glebe are crumbled as they often are,
The various kinds of grass and corn and leaves
Hiding in tiny form
These should be seen scattered among the clods of earth.
And when a fragment from a log is broken off
Then should smoke and ash and tiny flames be seen.
The facts will clearly show it does not happen so at all,
That thing in thing is not so mixed,
But rather atom forms, common to many things,
Lurk mingled in these things in various ways.
But often you will say, on lofty hills,
The tops of two tall trees grown side by side
Together rub—under compulsion of the strong south wind,
Until a flame has flashed, a flower of fire is born.
And yet I'm sure that you must know
That flame is not implanted in the wood,
But many seeds of heat,
Which flow together through the friction of the trees
And start a fire through all the woods.
But if the flame had lurked there ready made
The fire could not be hid for very long,
But burn the forests all at once, consume the trees to ash.
But don't you see the truth of what I said a little while before
The most important fact is this—
With just what atoms, atom forms combine,
And how they're placed, what interchange of motion they both give
                                                              and take.

And from this atom stuff with little change,
Timber or flame alike can come.

Just as in spelling when the order's changed of letters in a word,
Two different things result—timber and fire.
And now to sum it up.
If you suppose that objects visible and clear to view
Can never come to be without inventing primal principles of matter
                                                                    similar,
Assuming this your primal principles will die away,
Or rather they'd guffaw with quivering merriment,
And wet their face and chins with salty tears.

Fame is the spur

COME hear the rest, come lend your ears
To more prophetic strain.
I know how difficult my topic is.
Fame is the spur that touched my heart with hope
And branded breast with burning love of Muses.
Touched with Fame's spur, I feel my spirit glow;
I tread the trackless heights,
Not trodden earlier by foot of man.
I love to press towards unsullied rills and drink.
I love to pluck fresh flowers and weave
A splendid garland for my head,
In those rare heights whence ne'er before
The Muse has plucked a flower for any man.
My fame is this—I touch a mighty theme
And burst religion's bonds from human minds.
Then, too, I write on murky theme translucent verse
And coat on everything the Muse's charm.
In this, I think, I'm not unreasonable.
As doctors do when they give horrid drugs to boys,
First smear the glass around with honey's golden sweet.
The child's young age, detecting no deceit,
Drinks goodness down in bitter guise.

He's cheated, not betrayed.
Rather he's turned to health again.
Just this do I.
To some who have not tasted it,
This creed of mine may seem too grim.
Too many shrink away from it.
And so I wanted to expound for you
Deep wisdom in Pierian song
And coat the bitter drug of reason with the Muse's charm.
In this way I might hope to hold your mind
To theme both high and hard,
Until you'd mastered nature's shape and form.

The universe is infinite

Now since I've shown
That solid particles of atom stuff
Can ever flit about through endless time,
And quite unvanquished by the power of time,
Now let's enquire
Whether there's limit to their sum or not.
Then too the void we've found in which all things go on,
Let's see if void is bounded in,
Or stretches out in space quite limitless
In depth immeasurably great.
The sum of things I say is no wise limited,
In no direction that it goes.
For if it had a limit it must have an outer edge.
Now nothing can have an outer edge
Unless there's something further out to hem it in,—
A place beyond the power of sense to follow it.
But as things are, since this we must confess,
That nothing is beyond the sum of things,
The sum cannot have an end, limit or bound.

It matters not at all,
In what part of the whole you take your stand.
Whatever place a man takes up,
He leaves the whole as infinite on every side.
Suppose the opposite, imagine finite space.
Imagine running to the end, to furthest coasts,
Hurling a flying dart.
Would you suppose this dart when hurled with might and main,
Follows its path and flies afar,
Or would you think that something checks and bars its way?
For one of these alternatives you must admit and choose.
Yet both alternatives will hem you in, make you admit,
The whole is infinite.
For whether something checks it, keeps it from its goal,
Or if the dart keeps moving on its journey infinite,
In either case it starts not from the boundary of the universe.
But I'll press on, enquire,
Where'er you place the farthest coasts of universe,
What happened to the dart?
A boundary to things will ne'er be set,
And chance for further flight prolongs the flight
For evermore.
Then too if all the space in all the universe
From all sides were shut in
Were made with boundaries definite,
The sum of matter in the whole of things
Together would have flowed with solid weight
From every side and reached the bottom of the universe;
Then nothing would go on beneath the canopy of sky—
There'd be no sky at all nor heaven's light
The whole material sum of things would lie in idleness
Piled stack on stack,
By falling endlessly through time's infinity.

But as it is assuredly,
No rest is granted to the atom stream
Because there is no bottom to the universe
Where atom forms can flow together, find their rest.
In endless motion all things carry on from every side.
From beneath the atoms are stirred up, supplied from endless space.
And lastly, of the things we see before our eyes,
One thing is always boundary to the next.
For air walls in the hills and hills the air;
Land bounds the sea, the sea again all lands.
Nothing outside can be a boundary to the universe.
Space then, and void's immense profundity
Can not be traversed by the shining thunderbolt,
As this darts through the never ending tract of time.
Nor can it, in its course, reduce the span of space.
So far on every side spreads out the span of void's infinity—
In all directions, free from limit everywhere.
Nature herself has made the sum of things
Powerless to set a limit to itself.
For nature has decreed
That matter must by space be limited
And space by matter equally.
And so by alternation of the two
Nature has made the cosmos infinite.
Or should one fail, the other then
Spreads out immeasurable with Nature simple, pure.
(Were it not so)
Neither the sea, nor earth, nor shining temples of the sky,
Nor race of men, nor holy forms of gods
Could last a single hour.
For wrenched apart and kept from meeting of the atom particles
The stock of matter would be carried on through endless space;
Or rather freed from possibility of union,

It never could ensure that anything might come to be.
Assuredly it was not design, sagacious mind, creative deity
That made the atoms place themselves in due array;
Nor did they sign a compact to dictate
What motion each should start.
Rather in numbers infinite they move in many ways,
Throughout the whole immense expanse of space,
They're beaten and they're buffeted,
From infinite time in blind experiment essay
All movements and all meeting
Until they come
To this exact arrangement of atomic shapes
From which the present sum of things created stands.
And this same sum,
Preserved from harm through many mighty years
(When once for all to fitting motions atom forms have made their
way)
Brings the results that now you see—
The streams replenish greedy sea with copious water from their
springs,
And Mother Earth, fostered by heat of sun,
Renews her teeming brood,
And all the race of living things is bred and flourishes
The gliding stars in heaven still survive.
This they could never do
Unless abundance of material stuff,
Could rise and rise from Time's infinity,
And let each thing when time is ripe renew its loss.
For just as living things when robbed of food,
Must lose their flesh and waste away,
So everything must be dissolved
When once supply of matter's sustenance,
(However from the turnpike it was turned aside)

Fails to arrive.
And no external blows from every side
Can keep the universe once formed
Untouched by harm.
The atom stream can hammer at a portion of the universe,
Delay the process of its breaking up,
Till other blows succeed, until the sum of things can be supplied.
But oftentimes in spite of this creative atom swerve,
The atoms are compelled to bounce away again
And time and space alike are lavished on the atom stream,
To fly away again, avoid collisions, fail to unite.
And so again, again, I say
Atoms must always rise in infinite multitude
And that creative atom clash must never fail.
There must be matter limitless on every side.

Do not think that all things tend towards the centre

Now this false argument which some adduce,
I'd wish that Memmius heed not.
They say that all things strive towards the centre of the universe
And for this cause the world stands fast
Without external blows;
Bottom and top, they say, can never be resolved
Because all things must strive towards the centre of the universe.
(As though you could believe
That anything could stand upon itself.)
And that the heavy things beneath the earth press up,
Find their position upside down on earth,
Like images reflected in still pools;
And, if you please, they hold,
That living things walk upside down on earth
And cannot fall from earth and fly through space,
No more than we can freely fly through sky.

And when they see the sun, then we behold
The stars of night.
They share alternately the seasons of the sky.
Their nights are like our days.
But blind and empty blundering begets ideas like these; for fools.
Because they grasp ideas with twisted thought.
There cannot be a centre of the world,
Since universe is infinite.
And if there were a centre to the world,
Nothing there could rest.
For room and space which we call void,
Whether through centre, whether not
Must yield to heavy objects equally
Wherever tend the motions of the atom forms.
Nor is there any place, to which when atoms come,
They lose the influence of gravity and stand still in the void.
Nor can this empty space support a thing,
But quickly yields as nature of the void dictates.
And so it cannot be that things are forced to join in unity
Because they strive to reach the centre of the universe.
And furthermore the Stoics think,
That not all bodies strive to reach the centre equally
But only forms of earth and moisture—the waters of the sea,
And streams from mighty mountain tops,
And all the things we find enclosed in earthly frame.
But unsubstantial breezes of the air, they think,
And red hot fires,
Are outward borne from centre of the universe.
That for this cause,
The sky around is always twinkling with unnumbered stars
The flame of sun is fed through heaven's blue expanse,
Because the heat in headlong flight from centre of the universe,
Is gathered there.

The topmost boughs of trees, they think,
Could not bear leaves,
Unless from earth the food for each were raised and step by step.
But if their theory's true,
Then is the danger great,
That like the wingéd way of flame,
The ramparts of the universe should fly apart,
In sudden crash throughout the mighty void;
And all the rest of universe should follow them,
And all the thundering temples of the sky above should fall,
The earth in frenzied haste withdraw beneath our feet
And mid the tangled ruins of earth and sky,
Bodies of all created things be wrecked,
Depart through void profound,
That in a point of time no wreckage might be left behind,
Except deserted space and unseen atom forms.
Whichever side you think will be the first to fail
This is the gate of death for things.
On this side all the store of matter hurls itself abroad.
So led along by tiny toil,
All this you'll come to learn.
For first one thing grows clear and then the next.
Nor can black night obscure your path
Until you see,
The last great secret hiding place of Nature's laws,
As one thing sheds a light on other things.

Book Two

The joy and peace that comes from physical philosophy

O SWEET IT IS when on the mighty sea,
  The wind stirs up great billows,
One's own foot firm on steady earth,
To watch another's troubles.
Not that we find delight in others' strugglings,
But that its sweet to look on ills
From which oneself escapes.
Sweet, too, to look
When cavalcades of war contend upon the plain,
And one is safe, oneself.
But far surpassing everything in bliss it is
To occupy the high, serene, embattled eminence,
The ivory tower,
Whose muniments are thought and high philosophy,
The wisdom of the wise.
Here you look down and see, like tiny ants,
Men scurry to and fro, wandering here and there
Seeking to find the hidden path of life,
Well spent, well-ordered.
You see them battle with their wits,
Pit lineage 'gainst lineage,
Working day and night with sinews and with mind,

48

To gain the crown of wealth, the pride of power.
Men's wretched minds, men's blinded hearts!
In darkness deep, in peril sore,
This little life of ours is passed.
Not to see that Nature asks for nothing
But that, body free from pain and mind from care,
We can enjoy sweet peace of mind and spirit.
Few things we see our body really needs—
Enough to keep us free from pain.
Though these few things can serve up many luxuries—
Pleasant enough at times,
Nature does not need that,
If gilded effigies in sumptuous halls
With flaming torches in their raised right hands
Do not bring light to midnight feasts;
If gold and silver shimmer not and glint;
If music echo not from panelled and from gilded beams.
Without all these, in grassy nook reclined,—
A stream, a shady tree instead of luxury—
Needing no wealth, men tend their bodies' needs
And find sufficient bliss,
Spring on the mountains, flowers in every mead.
Tortured by sickness and by fever racked,
Does woven tapestry or deep rich purple glow
Bring healing quicker, as a bed, than peasant's cloak?
And so, since neither fame nor family nor wealth,
Can heal your body, can they help your mind?
Unless perhaps when your own legions strengthen self esteem
(You see them marching swift on open plain in mimic war,
Strengthened with great reserves and power of cavalry),
(You judge them both alike in arms, in spirit like),
In face of all their strength do superstitious fears
Flee headlong from the mind?

Does martial strength banish the fear of death,
Leave mind relaxed, or spirit free from tension?
But if we see that martial strength is only trivial mockery,
That really human fears and carking cares,
Dread not the clash of arms, the javelin flight,
And boldly move mid kings and high estate,
Bend not the knee before the sheen of gold,
Nor reverence rich tailorings of sumptuous cloth,
How can you doubt that freedom from external things
Is sovereign gift of reason?
Is not all life in darkness spent?
Like tiny boys who tremble in the dark
And think that anything may come,
We, also, tremble in the light,
And shrink from things that, in themselves, are no more terrible
Than what boys fear in dreams and fancy sure to be.
And so this darkened terror of the mind
Must be dispelled
Not by the rays of sun, the gleaming shafts of day
But nature's laws, by looking in her face.

*What movement of the atom stuff made things
And broke them down again when made*

COME now, I will unfold and tell
What movement of the atom stuff made things
And broke them down again when made,
And what compulsion's brought to bear on them,
And what velocity's assigned to them,
To fall through mighty void.
You lend attentive ears.
We surely know,
That matter does not cling close packed.
We see a thing grow small in lapse of time

And flow away as in a stream
When age removes it from our eyes;
And yet the sum of things remains the same.
The reason is
That bodies moving from a thing diminish what they left
Augment the thing to which they come.
The one grows old, the other waxes strong.
Yet even with the new they don't remain eternally.
And so the sum of things is ever new
And all things mortal live by give and take.
The generations wax, the generations wane;
In time's brief span all living things are changed,
Like runners in a race pass on life's torch.
Now if you think
That atom stuff can stand quite still
And standing still create new movements in the world of things
You're very wrong.
For since the atoms wander through the void
They either move by their own weight
Or else from impulse of the other atoms striking them.
For in their motion atom forms have often met and clashed
And so they leap apart—this way and that.
Nor is this wonderful,
For atoms are of stuff most hard with solid weight,
And nothing can withstand them in the rear.
The more you contemplate the atoms tossing here and there
The more you'll bring to mind
There is no bottom to the whole vast universe
No place for atom stream to rest,
Since space is limitless and stretches far on every side.
All this I've shown in many words
And proved with reasoning acute.
Since this is true

No rest is there for atoms moving through the mighty void,
But rather harassed as they are with motion endless and diverse
Some, when they clash, leap far apart in mighty intervals
Others a small way only from the blow.
And when the unity of atom forms is close
When atoms only leap a little way apart
(Because entangled by their own close-locking shapes)
These constitute the hardy roots of rock,
The savage bulk of iron and other things like that.
But of the rest which wander through the mighty void
A few leap far apart and leave great space between.
Now these create thin air, and shining light of sun.
But many wander through unending space
And have no chance
To meet and link themselves with other atom forms,
Or unify their moves with theirs.
Of these lone atoms, just as I've said
An image and a likeness ever turns
And presses on our eyes.

*The motes that dance in the sunlight illustrate the restless move-
ment of the atoms*

FOR think,
When rays of sun pour light through darkened house
Why then you'll see
A million tiny particles mingle in many ways
And dance in sunbeams through the empty space,
As though in mimic war the particles wage everlasting strife—
Troop ranged 'gainst troop, nor ever call a halt;
In constant harassment
They're made to meet and part.
So you can guess from this
Just what it means

That atoms should be always buffeted in mighty void.
And so,
A little thing can give a hint of big
And offer traces of a thought.
And so it's very right
That you should turn your mind to bodies dancing in the rays of sun;
Movements like this will give sufficient hint
That clandestine and hidden bodies also lurk,
In atom stream.
For if, you watch the motes
When dancing in a sunbeam you will often see
The motes by unseen clashings dashed to change their course,
Sometimes turn back, when driven by external blows
And whirl, now this way, then now that
Dancing every way at once.
So you may know
They have this restlessness from atom stream.
For first the atoms move themselves
And then the bodies which result from union of the few
Are near (if I can use such words) atomic power,
Are not embarrassed by the unseen blows of atom forms.
And they in turn
Stir up the larger complexes of things
And so the chain of movement passes upward from the atom stream
And bit by bit comes forth to meet our sense,
Until those bodies move which we can see
Clear in the light of sun;
Yet none the less the blows by which they move are never seen.

The speed with which the atoms move

AND now the speed assigned atomic particles
In phrases few, my friend, you learn from this;
First when the Lady of the Dawn

Has strewn the lands with early light
And divers birds flitting through distant woods
Through ether soft, fill all the land with liquid cries
It's evident for all to see
How swiftly rises sun to clothe and flood all things with light.
And yet the heat of sun, its light serene,
Does not cross empty space
And so it has to go more slow and break through waves of air.
And too,
The various particles of heat do not move one by one
But closely tangled in a close knit mesh.
One holds the other back, impedes it from without
And so they move more slow.
But atoms, as I've said, are solid in their singleness
And when these pass through void and nothing checks them from
                                                        without
But, made as they are, a unity from different parts
They press toward the spot which first they sought to reach,
These must surpass the light of sun in speed,
Be faster borne along and traverse many times the space in equal
                                                        time
Than sun, which floods the sky with light.
And yet, against all this, a certain sect
Because it's ignorant of matter's power
Believe that, not without the help of gods,
Could Nature change the seasons of the year, create the crops,
So nicely tempered to the needs of men
And all the other things create besides
Which pleasure, Divinest force, persuades men to approach
Pleasure, that guide of human life,
Pleasure, that leads men on
Through artifice of Venus to renew their race,
That mankind perish not.

But when these men suppose
That gods have ordered everything for sake of man
It's clear they're very far from truth.
Though I knew nothing of the atom stream,
Yet this I would affirm from looking at the working of the sky
And prove by many other things as well
That nature was not made for men by grace divine.
It holds too many flaws.
This I'll make clear to you, my friend, a little later on.
But now I must expound what else there is to tell of atom stream.

Atoms are subject to the force of gravity and always stream downwards

THIS is the place, I think, to prove to you
That bodies cannot move upward by themselves,
Of their own power.
I fear lest flame deceive you here.
It's true that smiling crops and trees
Are born and grow towards the sky
Although all things by weight are downward borne;
And flames rush up to meet the roof
And swiftly play on rafters and on beams
But must we think that they do this spontaneously,
Without some driving force?
Just as when blood pours from a wound
And spurts on high and scatters carnage round:
Do you not see
How water pushes beams and rafters up most forcefully.
The more we push them down again—
Many of us at once
The more it spews them up and sends them back
And from the water they will rise and stand on end.
And yet we do not doubt, as I believe,

That all these things press down so far as in them lies,
And are always carried downward through the void.
And equally do flames, when forced by pressure from without
Rise upward through the airy breeze
Although their weight is fighting, too, to bring them down.
Again the nightly torches of the sky, the meteors,
Drag endless tracks of flame across the sky
Whenever nature sends them on their way.
You see the stars and constellations fall to earth?
The sun, too, from its lofty height in sky,
Scatters its heat on every side and sows the field with light:
Down to the earth the sun's heat makes its way.
And thunderbolts fly crosswise through the rain,
And now from this side, now from that, fires burst from the cloud,
Rush to unite.
The impetus of flame is almost always to the earth.

The swerve of the atoms

I LONG that you should grasp this point, too, in our search.
When atoms fall straight downward through the void,
Impelled by their own weight,
At some chance time and some chance intervals in space,
They swerve a bit,
So slightly that you scarce can call it swerve.
Unless they did, eternally straight down they'd fall
Like raindrops in a storm.
Unless they did,
There'd be no clash nor clinging in the atom stream.
Nothing could nature ere create.
If any think
That weightier atoms swifter through the void are borne
And hence come movements which give shape to things,
In this he's clearly wrong.

When objects fall straight down through water or thin air,
The heavier faster falls, just because the medium
Checks not all things in equal measure equally,
But rather faster yields to heavier things.
And empty space can never, anywhere, check things in flight.
Its nature makes it yield.
And so both heavy things and light
Are borne at equal pace through silent void.
The heavy cannot strike the light by swifter flight,
Nor cause the clashes nor the variant motion—
Nature's way of making things.
And so, once more, once more, I moved to say
Atoms must swerve the tiniest bit.
If not we're forced to think that bodies sideways fall—
They clearly don't.
This is apparent, this is manifest,
That bodies, of themselves, can never sideways move;
But fall straight down, as you yourself can see.
But who is there who sees that nothing ever swerves
From straight-down movement of its perpendicular path?
Once more, if movement always is to other movement linked
And if the new comes ever from the old,
As in determinist argument;
If atoms in their swerve do not fresh start
To break the bonds of Fate;
If cause may follow cause from infinite time,
Whence comes free will for living things on earth?
Whence comes this power, I say, snatched from the grasp of Fate
This Will whereby we move wherever fancy prompts?
For move we do
At no fixed times and no fixed intervals of space,
Wherever mind suggests.
Assuredly, at times like these,

Man's purpose is the starting point;
His purpose stirs the motion in his limbs.
You've seen on race track, when the barriers down,
The eager strength of racing horse
Cannot set limbs in motion half so fast
As eager mind conceives.
The total sum of matter through the frame
Must be aroused, and so stirred up
That every limb may follow mind's swift prompting.
So you may see
The start of motion comes from out the heart;
The mind's firm will gives it the starting point.
And thence it spreads through all the frame and limbs.
It's not the same at all
As if we were to move,
Kicked forward by a mighty blow,
And mighty outside force.
For then it's clear to see
Our bulky body moves, is pushed along against our will,
Until the will has reined it back
And checked the force through all our limbs.
And so you see
That though a force outside has often pushed a man and made him
move
Against his will,
Yet there is still a power within the man
That fights against external force and holds it back,
And at the bidding of this inner power
The matter of our limbs and joints
Is sometimes made to turn,
And though pushed on by force outside
Is reined and stopped
And made to come to rest again.

And so you must admit
That in the atom stream there is another cause,
Not only blows and weights which move things from without
And from this other cause there comes
This inborne power in us
(Since nothing comes to be from nothing by divine decree).
For weight it is you know by whose decree
All things can not be brought to be by blows outside,
By some external force.
But that the mind feels free,
Is not constrained by force within from doing what it does
Is not a helpless prisoner of war,
To suffer and endure,
All this results,
From that first tiny atom swerve
At no fixed time and no fixed interval of space.

The conservation of matter and motion

THE total stock of matter was not in days of old more dense,
Nor looser packed with greater intervals
Than now it is.
For nothing ever comes to join the total stock
Nor leaves,
To lessen or increase its store.
The atoms through the ages past
Moved as now they do;
And even so they'll move eternally.
And what before was wont to come to be
Will come to be again by laws the same;
Exist and grow, be strong and flourishing
So far as Nature's laws permit.
No force can change the sum of things.
There's nothing left beyond the boundaries of the universe

To which the atoms might escape,
Nor whence a force might rise and burst into the world,
To alter all the motions of the universe and change its basic laws.

The constant motion of the atom stream

Now this you need not wonder at,
Nor ask the reason why
Though all the atoms are in constant restless motion stirred
The sum of things seem still.
(Unless, of course, some individual thing
Starts movements in its own particular frame).
For all the movements of the atom particles
Lie far from sense and rest below the view.
We cannot see atomic particles;
Why wonder that their movements are hidden from our eyes?
For many things that we *can* look upon
Still hide their movement when they're far away.
For often fleecy flocks
Crop the lush pastures on a distant hill.
And every sheep creeps on wherever sight of tempting pasture sum-
                                                    mons him;
Or grass with jewels of dew,
While tiny lambs, their bellies full, butt playfully.
And yet from far, all this seems blurred
And seems to lie a single mass of white,
On far green hill.
And then again when mighty legions fill the spaces of the plain
Stirring up mimic war,
The sheen of weapons reaches to the sky
And all the air is filled with flash of bronze;
The earth beneath is filled with noise—
The clamor made by mighty mass of marching men;
The mountains smitten by the sound

Echo the warriors' shouts to stars of firmament;
The horsemen wheel and in a sudden charge
Make the plains shake with torrent of their headlong speed.
And yet to one observing from a lofty eminence,
High in the hills,
All seems to rest, all seems to lie a solid gleaming mass upon the plain.

Variety of atom shapes

COME now, in order learn of atoms, how diverse they are,
How differently they're formed with differing shapes.
Not in the sense that few are like in form,
But generally they're not everywhere, not all alike.
Nor should we wonder; atoms so many, atoms limitless,
Need not always, everywhere, be similar in size and shape.
Then, too, the race of men,
The voiceless, scaly fish that swim the seas,
Glad herds, wild beasts, the various birds
Which haunt the joyful banks, the springs, the pools,
That flit through distant glades,
Take any one you want as specimen;
You'll find it differs slightly from its kind.
This, too, is how a child can know its mother; mother, child.
We know they can and beasts no less than men.
Often outside the lovely shrines of gods
On incense—breathing stone of altar,
A calf is slain.
Its breast pours out a hot and reeking stream of blood.
Its mother in her loss wanders the grassy glades
And seeks the footprint in the ground of tiny cloven hoof.
And everywhere she turns her longing eyes for sight of loved one lost.
Again she stands and fills the leafy glades with loud lament;
Often comes back to old familiar stall,

In hope to find him.
Her heart is pierced with yearning for her loved one lost.
Nor can green willows or the dew fresh grass,
Nor old familiar streams up level with their banks,
Bring joy to heart or heal the pang of loss.
The sight of other calves in meadows lush helps not.
Thus every creature loves and needs its own;
Horned goats are recognized by tiny kids with tremulous bleating.
Butting lambs in pasture know their mother's call.
Nature demands that each return for milk to mother's udder.
Grains, too, kind by kind, are never quite alike.
Take any one you want as specimen,
You'll find it differs slightly from its kind.
The same in shells that paint the lap of earth,
Where sea with gentle waves
Beats on the thirsty sand of winding shore.
And so I must insist these things must be;
The atoms are by nature made, not all alike,
Not turned out in the mass in some dark factory.
Differ then they must.
Now why the fire of heaven's lightening more piercing is by far
Than that of ours which flows from torch of pine on earth,
This riddle's easy for the mind to read.
The heavenly fire you'd say is made of smaller atom shapes,
Atoms more subtle and more fine.
And so this fire can pass through openings
That fire on earth, rising from logs and offspring of the resin brand
Can never pass.
And light can pass through lantern's horn while water is repelled.
Atoms of light are smaller far than those which constitute the foster-
ing liquid stream.
And wine will swiftly through a strainer run
While sluggish olive oil holds back.

The atoms of the olive oil must larger be
More hooked and more entangled each with each.
And so the nexus of the atom particles can not be drawn apart
One from the rest and each one make its way
Through single holes of things.
Then too,
The liquid juice of honey and the warm sweet milk
Are pleasant to the tongue when tasted in the mouth.
But wormwood foul and bitter centaury
Pucker the mouth with loathsome taste.
The pleasant tasting things are made from atom particles
Both smooth and round;
The bitter tasting things are made of atoms hooked
That tear a way by force through organs of the sense,
And break our body as they enter in.
And last of all
Things that the senses find both good and bad
Are mutually at war,
Because, you see
They're made from atoms of a different shape.
And so you must not think
The bitter horror of the piercing saw
Is made of particles as smooth
As melodies of music which the skilled musicians wake,
Shaping the notes while fingers nimbly run across the strings.
Nor must you think again
That atoms like in shape can pierce the nose
When men burn corpses on a funeral pyre
As when the theatre stage is dewed with saffrons from Cilicia,
While neighbouring altars breathe the scent
Of frankincense from Araby.
Nor can you think
That pleasant colours—those which feed the eyes

Are made from self same atom stuff
As those which prick the pupils, those which make us weep,
Foul sights and horrible to see.
For every shape which ever charms our sense
Has not been brought to be without some smoothness in its atom
stuff.

Or every sharp, offensive shape
Without some roughness in its atom stuff.
And other atoms, too, we must suppose
Not wholly smooth, not, altogether hooked with jagged points
Are made with tiny angles standing out a bit.
And substance made from these
Can gently tickle, stimulate our sense, not hurt.
Examples I can give—the lees of wine or endive's taste.
Again that heat of fire and cold of frost
Have atoms differing in their shape is proved to us by touch.
For touch, ye holy gods, yes, touch
Is sense supreme, the bodies chiefest instrument
When something strikes it from outside
Or when a pain born in the body gives us hurt
Or pleasure in the body born
Creates delight in passing out
As men all know from love's creative act.
Sometimes the atoms by one another roused
Disturb our sense.
If by chance you've struck some other part of body with your hand
You'll know of this; this serves for an experiment.
And so it has to be that atoms very differently are shaped
To bring about such various feelings in our sense.
Once again, things which seem hard, compact
Are made of atoms far more closely hooked
Are held more closely at their roots
(If such a metaphor I dare to use)

By branching particles.
Of things like these the diamond takes its stand in vanguard rank.
It's schooled to disregard, despise all blows;
And after diamonds come the stubborn flints, the strength of iron,
Sockets of brass which scream aloud
In struggle with the bolts.
Now certain things are made from atoms smooth and round,
Liquids, I mean.
A heap of poppy seed moves easily
Just like a drink of water.
The smooth round heap of poppy seeds
Will never hold together;
And when struck, the seeds roll down the hill like water.
And all the things which fly asunder instantly,
Like smoke and clouds and flame,
Such things are not completely made of atoms smooth and round;
And yet the structure of their atom stuff,
Is not close packed.
The human body they can wound, penetrate rocks
Without to one another clinging close.
And so the prickliness assigned to them
Consists of pointed not of tangled atom stuff.
Nor need you wonder that some fluid things are bitter too.
The brine of sea will serve to illustrate.
The fluid in the sea is made of atoms smooth and round,
But many painful, rugged ones are mingled in;
And yet they're not together held by hooks.
And rugged though they are they still are round,
That's how they roll together, hurt the human sense.
Now that you may the more believe
That atoms smooth and rough are mixed,
From these the bitter body of the sea god made,
It's not so hard to separate the two and see yourself.

For when the water trickles through the earth,
The fresh comes through, the salt remains behind.
The rougher particles, you see, will always cling to earth.

The number of the atom shapes is limited

Now since I've taught so much,
I'll hasten to conjoin a truth
That's fitted close to what I've said,
And wins belief from it.
Atoms, I hold are limited in number of their shapes.
Were it not so
Then many atoms must be infinite in size.
Within one tiny atom frame
The number of the shapes could not be so diverse.
Assume that atom forms possess three tiny parts
Or add a few more, if you wish;
And now arrange these parts in various ways
And shift them top to bottom, left to right,
And find what shape the various arrangements give the whole.
Now, if you desire, to make a change and shift their shape,
You must add other parts.
This new arrangement then will ask for other parts
If still a new shape you'd create.
And so increase of bulk must follow newness in the forms
Nor can you believe
That atoms are endowed with infinite varieties of shape
Lest you imagine some of huge extent.
And this I've shown above is quite impossible.
For then you'd see barbaric robes and gleaming cloth
Dyed with the purple from the shells of Thessaly,
Purple that imitates the golden peacocks—dipped in laughing charm,
Neglected and surpassed by colours new.

66

That mighty earth must rest on air;
That earth can never rest on earth.
And to her car they linked the savage beasts to signify
That beasts however wild must by a parent's loving care
Be tamed and softened.
And on her head they placed a crown of battlements
Because, enthroned on glorious heights, she nurtures towns.
And so endowed with this majestic symbolism
Her statue to this day is borne in state through lands of mighty folk.
And various peoples call on her
As Mother of Ida.
Now Phrygian bands they give to keep her company
Because tradition says from Phrygia,
Grain was at first produced and spread through all the world.
And eunuch priests were given her
To signify that those who flaunt the goddess' sanctity
Or those who to their parents failed in gratitude
Are found unfit to bring their living offspring to the shores of light.
Taut timbrels thunder in their hands
With hollow cymbals all around
Trumpets with menace and harsh sounding bray,
The hollow pipe that stimulates their minds
In Phrygian mode.
Weapons they hold in front of them to symbolize their mad and
                                        dangerous mood,
To fill with fear, through power divine,
The thankless minds, the impious hearts of sullen multitude.
And as she rides through mighty towns
And sheds her silent benediction over men
They strew her path with silver and with bronze
And dedicate their bounteous alms;
Goddess alike, and those attending her,
Are strewn with roses—thick as snowflakes in a driving storm.

And then an arméd band, whom Greeks Curétes call
Sporting mid Phrygian troops, leaping in rhythmic ecstasy
Rejoice at sight of blood and shake the dreadful crests upon their
heads.

Their name recalls the ancient Cretan band
Who drowned the wailing of the infant Jove—
A band of boys surrounds the baby boy—
And beat on measured rhythm, brass clashing on brass,
The while they prayed,
That Saturn might not find him, seize him, tear him with all-power-
ful jaws,
Inflict eternal wound, deep in the Mother's heart.
So this is why with arms they follow Cybele;
Or else perhaps her teaching they exemplify
That men with arms and courage high should guard their Father-
land
And be a guard and glory for their sires.
Yet all of this,
Though nobly told and splendidly set forth
Is very far from truth.
The gods must pass their lives in everlasting peace
Their interests far removed from this our world.
The gods through all eternity
Are free from danger, free from grief,
Majestic in their self-sufficiency.
They do not need mankind at all.
The gods are not seduced by piety;
Never are gods by anger stirred.
The great round world is not endowed with consciousness,
But, owning many atom forms,
It can bring forth such varied things so variously to light of sun.
Of course, if you must instead of sea
Say Neptune;

72

Instead of grain, invoke the goddess Ceres as its patroness;
Or pray to Bacchus, rather than speak of wine,
Why then, we can't object if one proclaims,
Earth as the Mother of the Gods.
Only not let him stain his mind with grovelling
Or foul religious awe.

The differences in species and in things reflect the difference in their atom forms

BUT now returning to the atom stream;
The fleecy flocks, the warrior breed of horse
Horned herds that crop the grass from fields the same
Beneath the same vast arching canopy of sky,
Assuage their burning thirst from self same streams
Yet live their various lives, and keep the form
And imitate their father's ways, kind after kind.
So great the difference in atom forms,
In any grass you will, in any stream.
Now every living creature of them all
Is made of blood and veins and bones and heat,
Sinews and moisture—in a word of flesh.
All these are quite unlike
As made of atoms differing in shape.
Again all things that burn, that blaze with fire
Hold in themselves at least those atom forms
That cause a fire; which let them shoot abroad
Both light and heat and make sparks fly
And scatter cinders far and wide.
Now range through other things with piercing power of mind.
You'll find the same.
All hold within themselves the seeds of many things—
Atoms of different shapes.
And certain things have colour, taste and smell assigned to them—

73

A prime example, fruits.
Now these must be of different atom forms.
The smell can pierce our members; colour cannot.
But both in different ways can find a passage to our consciousness.
And so you know, they differ in their atom shapes.
Thus various atom forms make up one mass
And things are made with mingled seeds.
Why even in this verse of mine you'll find
A lot of letters, common to many words.
And yet,
Verses and words are made from different letters of the alphabet.
A few of these, it well may be, are seen in all of them;
And two of them may be composed of letters quite the same,
And yet they all can't be alike.
And so with things.
There may be atoms common to objects, quite a few,
And yet create a different sum.
And so it's right to say—
The human race and corn and smiling trees
Are made of different forms.
Nor must we think
That all the atoms can be joined in all the several ways.
For if they were you'd see
All kinds of monstrous things emerge.
Creatures you'd see half human and half beast
Or lofty boughs of trees emerge from the body of an animal;
Or limbs from beasts terrestial joined to the beasts of sea.
And Nature, too, throughout the lands—
The lands—
The universal parents of created things
Feeding Chimaeras
Creatures that breathe out flame from noisome mouths.
But clearly none of these can come to be

Since all things grow from atom forms assigned
With parents fixed,
With law ordained how each should grow, preserve its species and its
kind.
For each thing finds its proper atoms separate from every kind of food
And these pass to the limbs, with other atoms there are linked
And institute the proper movements through the whole.
Alien matter, too is dashed by nature to the ground.
And many atom forms
Recoil unseen from human frame driven away by constant blows
For these could not find link to any part
Nor living motions feel in harmony with human frame
Or imitating it.
Not living things alone. All things are limited by this same law.
For all created things must differ utterly
And this is proof they're made of atom forms of different shapes.
(Some are, of course, alike but never all.)
With atoms differing—there must also be
A difference in their spaces, ways and fastenings,
Their weight and blows, their meetings, movements,
All the differences which sunder living things,
Which sunder even more
The earth from sky, the sky from sea.

Secondary qualities of the atoms. Atoms are colorless

COME now and listen to the doctrine amassed by pleasant toil of
mine.
I would not have you think that objects white which gleam before our
eyes
From atoms white are made;
Or objects black are made from atoms black;
Or any other coloured thing you will,
Are made from atom forms with hue the same.

75

Atoms, indeed, are colourless—
Not like or unlike the things to which they're made.
And if you thing the onslaught of the intellect
Can not project itself within, attain to things like these
You're wandering far from truth.
Men are born blind, have never seen the light of sun,
And yet they comprehend the world around by touch—
From earliest infancy such men
Never associate colour with a thing.
From this you may infer
That bodies colorless may touch our sense.
And in blind darkness when we touch a thing,
It has no hue at all.
Now since I win conviction for this truth
We now agree that atom forms can have no hue.
For colour, whatsoever shade it be, must change,
But elemental principles should not behave like this;
There must be something that abides unchangeable
In order that the sum of things should not be brought to nothingness.
For whatsoever is changed, beyond its limit goes,
This straightway is the death of that which went before.
And so take care
You do not in imagination stain atomic forms with colour
Lest you find, this way,
The sum of things is brought to nothingness
Again if hue is not assigned to atom forms,
But differing shapes,
From which they can produce and vary
Colours of every kind
(Since often it's a matter of profound significance
With just what atoms other atoms join
And how they're placed, arranged
What motions they transmit, receive among themselves)

You easily can see
Why things which once were black like blackest ebony
Can rival suddenly
The shining whiteness of the marble stone.
Ocean will serve to illustrate;
When mighty winds have stirred its still expanse
Its waves are white as snow.
For when atomic shapes of that which generally seems black
Are stirred, the order changed, some added, some removed,
It straightway seems a gleaming white.
But if the atoms of the ocean waves were made of sky-blue seeds
They never could seem white;
No matter how you stir the atoms of a sky-blue tint
They never take the colour of the marble stone.
But if the atom forms which make the pure and unmixed colour of the
                                                                sea
Are dyed with various hues
(Even as often out of various forms and diverse shapes
A square is made—one single shape)
Just so it would be natural that we perceive in Ocean's depths
Or any other single, pure, unsullied sheen
Colours far different and diverse;
(Just as quite different forms make up the square.)
And more
The differing shapes do not prevent at all
The whole from being square,
Whereas the different colouring in things
Makes quite impossible
The single, simple brightness in a thing.
And so the reasoning which lures us on, entices us
To give a colour to atomic shapes
Is gone.
For white things are not made from atoms white

77

Nor black from black; but various.
More easily will white things come to be from atoms colourless
Than out of black or any colour which will fight with white
And block its way.
Then too,
Since colours cannot come to be without the help of light
And atom shapes can never come to light
From this you know
That atoms are not clothed, endowed with any colour.
What colour could there in darkness black?
Nay, colour itself is changed by light itself,
When things are struck with straight or slanting beams.
The plumage of the doves will illustrate this fact.
The feathered glory, set around their throats, crowning their necks
Gleams in the sunlight sometimes red with garnet hue
And sometimes emerald green, shot through with blue.
Again the peacock's tail is shot with varying hues,
Bathed in bright sun.
And since these various colours come to be with varying shafts of light
How can we divorce in thought
Colour from light?
And since the pupil of the eye
Accepts a certain kind of blow when it sees white
Another kind when it sees black;
And since it matters not at all
With just what colour things you touch have been endowed
But rather shape of atoms is the crucial thing
From this you know
That atoms have no need of hue
But by their various shapes produce the various things to touch.
Now since no colours fixed have been assigned to atom shapes
And any conformation of the atom forms can come in any hue
Why aren't the things that come from atom forms

Endowed in every kind with every kind of colour?
Nor were it strange in such a case
That flying crows should throw off white
That swans be black—from atoms black composed,
Or any other colour that you please—
Single or various.
And then,
The more a thing is pulled apart to tiny bits,
The more you see its colour
Fading away and quenched.
A piece of purple cloth will serve to illustrate;
The more you tear it up, unravel every thread,
The more the rich dark purple hue, the brightest colour in the uni-
                                                        verse,
Is brought to naught.
From this you know
The tiniest shreds of things must lose their hue
Before they break into the atom stuff of things.
Last argument;
Since you don't admit
That bodies all send out a smell or sound
From this it's clear
You don't think sound or smell inheres in them.
And even so
Since human eyes cannot discern all things
You know that some of them are made quite colourless
Some without sense, some far removed from sound,
And yet the eager mind can come to know these things
As easily as all the rest.

Secondary qualities of the atoms. They are without heat and cold.
Without sound, without odor, without moisture

Now, lest you think that colour is the only quality that atoms lack,
They're far removed from warmth and cold and fiery heat,

They move around, barren of sound and quite devoid of taste
No smell emit at all.
It's just as when you set to work to make a scent—delicious to the
nose
Assailing nostrils like the nectar of the gods
With whiff of marjoram or myrrh or spikenard
You first search out a scentless oil
That will not taint or spoil the perfume that you wish to make.
Exactly so, the atoms cannot bring a scent to things
Since they have none themselves—
Nor cold nor warmth nor fiery heat.
Yet since these qualites are made by man;
The pliant things of atoms soft,
The brittle with the atoms crumbling; hollow things of atoms rare—
All qualities must be thought removed from atom stuff
If we're to have immortal underpinning under things
On which the whole may rest.
Were it not so the whole wide world would pass away to nothingness.

Atoms are not endowed with consciousness

AND now you must admit
That all the things you see endowed with consciousness—
The power of sense,
Are made of atom stuff insensible.
The facts themselves, quite manifest for all to see
Do not refute or contradict this truth.
Rather they gently guide us by the hand and make us see
That living things have come to be
From atom stuff insensible.
Why we see worms emerge from noisome dung
When dewy earth is soaked to mud by torrents of tempestuous rain.
All other things in this way change.

Water from streams, and leaves and joyous grass
Transform themselves to be the flesh of grazing cows;
The flesh of beasts can make our human bodies grow,
And human flesh in turn can make the strength of savage beasts in-
                                                    crease,
And strong winged birds.
And so creative Nature changes food
To build the flesh of living things
And out of food begets all consciousness—
Just as she turns dry logs to flames, all things to fire.
Now don't you see the crucial nature of the atom stuff—
Order, position of the atom shapes,
And with what other atoms mixed
They move, are moved in turn?
And now we ask what forces strike the mind, compel the mind
To utter various thoughts.
Lest you should think the sensible were from insensate matter born.
We may be sure
That wood and earth and stones together mixed
Cannot make vital thought.
Remember this;
I do not say that out of all the movements that bring consciousness,
Consciousness is straightway born.
It matters much how big the bodies are that bring us consciousness
And what their shape and how arranged and placed and moved.
And none of these conditions can we see in logs or sod.
And yet when logs or turf are wet to saturation by the rains
They bring forth little worms.
This is because material atom forms,
Stirred from their old arrangement by the new
Find now the union out of which these primal living creatures can be
                                                    born.
.   .   .   .   (Text corrupt.)

For consciousness is always joined to sinews, flesh and veins
And these we see are always soft—with mortal form endowed.
And even if we grant
That these abide, endowed with immortality
Yet even so we have to think
They have the consciousness that's proper to a part,
Or else alternately
Must think them like to total living things.
But parts themselves cannot have consciousness.
For every moment of our human consciousness
Exists related to the total man.
The hand or other organ of the mortal frame if severed from the whole
Can never feel.
And so the parts
Must be like the whole.
Therefore the parts must feel, just as we feel,
And altogether share with us in every aspect of our consciousness.
How then can these be called first principles?
How shun the paths of death?
Since these are living things;
And living things are altogether mortal things.
Yet even if the parts could feel
Still by their meeting and their union
Nothing they make except a meeting and a crowd of living things.
For nor could herds of cattle, beasts or men
Bring forth another species from their casual jostling.
But if the atom stuff when once achieving consciousness
Should lose its own, achieve in turn another consciousness
How can it help at all that that be given them
Which formerly was snatched away?
And then there is the point we made before—
That eggs of birds turn into living chicks,

That worms swarm out of earth
When putrefaction grips the ground because of heavy rains.
From this we know that consciousness
Is able to emerge from atom stuff more primitive,
Not yet endowed with consciousness.
If anyone should argue this:
That consciousness can come to be from what is not endowed with
consciousness
By changing substance,
By (to use a metaphor) a kind of birth
By which the new creation—consciousness
Is thrust to be, exist;
To him we must reply, explain—
There cannot be a birth unless there was a previous union of the atom
stuff,
That nothing can be changed by some such union.
First we may be sure that nothing can have consciousness
Unless it lives.
Its atom stuff is scattered far abroad
Is held in air, in streams, in earth and things that spring from earth.
Not yet have atom forms combined the proper vital movements, each
with each
Whereby the all-percipient sense is formed
To guard the safety of each living thing.
Then too,
A heavier blow than each thing's nature can endure
Falling on any living thing
Will fell the creature, quickly stun the consciousness
Both in body and in mind.
Arrangement of the atom stuff is broken up,
The vital movements deep within are checked,
Until the shaking of the atom stuff
Deep, through all the limbs,

Breaks up the vital union of the soul,
And drives it out through every pore.
What could we think a blow accomplishes
When landing on a thing except to shatter it, break it to bits?
It often happens too
That when a lighter blow assails
The vital motions that remain can sometimes win,
So soothe the vast disturbance of the blow
And bring each part again back to its proper path
Shake, as it were, apart the move to death
That seemed to hold full sway,
And kindle once again the consciousness so nearly lost.
How else could living things regain their wits
And turn again to life
Just when they touch the gloomy gates of death,
Failing to reach the end of life.
Then too, when any substances of living things
Are moved by any force through flesh and limbs
And tremble deep within, each in its fixed abode,
The thing feels pain;
But when they settle down again
Gracious delight must make its way through every creature's frame.
From this you know,
That atoms in themselves cannot feel pain
Cannot find pleasure in and of themselves;
Since they're not unions of atomic stuff
By novel motion on the part of which the thing feels pain
Or gains the gracious fruit of sweet delight.
So atoms, we conclude are not endowed with consciousness.
But if, explaining feeling in a thing,
We *must* assign some consciousness to atom stuff
What of the things with which the race of men is specially endowed?
Do atoms shake with quivering mirth and laugh aloud

84

And sprinkle little atom's face and cheeks with laughter's tears?
And will these atom forms be smart enough
To utter many truths about the mixtures that compose the world?
Will these tiny atom forms go on to make profound research
Into the nature of atomic stuff?
For if the atoms were like mortal men in every point,
Then they must be composed of other particles in turn,
And these again of other particles.
You'll never dare to stop.
And here I must press home the argument.
Whatever you suppose can laugh and speak and think
Must be composed in turn of other particles,
That laugh and speak and think.
But if we once perceive that such a view is madness, sheer delirium,
And that a man can laugh
Even though he's not composed of laughing particles;
That man can think and reason with profoundest scholarship,
Though not composed of atoms eloquent and scholarly,
Why shouldn't creatures that have consciousness
Exist through union of the atom stuff itself insensible?

Now in this sense but in this sense alone,
We all are sprung from heavenly seed

Now in this sense, but in this sense alone,
We all are sprung from heavenly seed.
One Lord and Father is for all of us,
Great Father, Sky.
And when the bounteous Mother Earth has taken in herself
The watery drops of moisture from the Father, Sky,
She teems, and brings to birth the glorious crops,
The joyous shrubs, yes and the human race
And wild things in their various tribes she brings to birth

And furnishes the food on which their bodies feed
To live a pleasant life and propagate their kind.
And so, its right to call her Mother, Earth.
Exactly so,
What once has come from earth returns to earth
And what came down from sky,
Returns again to everlasting shores of sky.
And death does not destroy the stock of matter utterly
But only breaks the unions out of which all things are made.
But then again in turn they join in combinations new
And change their shapes and moderate their hues,
Receive sensations, give them up again,
Just in the twinkle of an eye.
So you may see the crucial meaning of the atom stuff,
Order, position of the atom shapes,
And with what other atoms mixed,
They move, are moved in turn;
Nor should you think
That all that's tossed up on the tide of time
And now is born, and now as swiftly dies,
Endures in its own self with endless, eternal atom stuff.
For even in this verse I write it makes a signal difference
How letters are combined and in what order they are placed.
The self same letters signify
The sky and sea and earth, rivers and sun,
And crops and trees and living things.
Most are alike—not all.
Arrangement makes them give their various sounds.
So it is likewise with atomic shapes
Their intervals and ways,
Their intermingling and their blows and weights,
Their meeting, movement, order and position, shape can change,
And in their changing, things change too.

AND now please turn your mind to true philosophy.
A doctrine new and wonderful is struggling to penetrate your ears,
A novel face of things to show itself.
For even the easiest truth must find it hard at first to win belief,
And nothing is so great and marvellous,
But bit by bit men fail to hold the thing in awe.
The bright clear colour of the sky, and all it holds,
The stars that wander here and there,
The moon and shining sun with glorious light
Suppose that human kind could see all this afresh, anew.
If unexpectedly this pageant of the universe
Were placed before their eyes
What story could be told more marvellous than this
To what could human kind be less inclined to lend
Prior belief?
This is my view:—
There's nothing could compare in wonder with a novel sight like
this.

And yet,
Sated and weary with the wonted sight
There's no one now who'll deign an upward glance,
Or gaze upon the shining temples of the sky.
So you,
Not struck with empty terror of the new
Spit not the glorious good of reason from your mind;
Rather with eager thought and judgment keen,
Weigh everything.
If you find it true then raise your hands and yield;
But if you find it false, prepare yourself to fight.
The human mind seeks truth.
Since space is infinite beyond the ramparts of the universe

It needs to know what lies afar in this infinity,
As far as human thought can penetrate,
As far as free assault of mind can range unchecked.
Now first I claim our search has shown;—
In all directions, everywhere,
On every side, above, below, through all the universe,
That space is infinite.
This I have shown; the truth of this must scream aloud,
The darkness of the deep abyss, shine clear.

There are many worlds

Now here is something we must not think probable
Since space is infinite on every side,
Since atoms numberless throughout the mighty universe
Fly here and there, by motion everlasting e'er impelled,
That this one world of ours, this earth and sky
Alone were brought to birth.
We cannot cherish this belief—
Beyond the confines of the world we know,
Nature does nothing.
Particularly as the world we know
Was made by Nature thus;—
The atoms of their own accord
Jostled from time to time by chance,
In random fashion, clashed, and blindly, heedlessly
And oft in vain,
Until at last were unions suddenly achieved
To be the starting points of mighty things,
Of earth and sea and sky, of every living thing.
And so I say again, again you must confess
That somewhere in the universe
Are other meetings of the atom stuff resembling this of ours;

And these the aether holds in greedy grip.
For when the atom stuff is there,
And space in which the atom stuff may move,
And neither thing nor cause to bring delay,
The process of creation must go on; things must be made.
Now as it is,
If atom stocks are inexhaustible,
Greater than power of living things to count,
If Nature's same creative power were present too
To throw the atoms into unions—exactly as united now,
Why then confess you must
That other worlds exist in other regions of the sky,
And different tribes of men, kinds of wild beasts.
This further argument occurs;
Nothing in nature is produced alone,
Nothing is born unique, or grows unique, alone,
Each thing is always specimen—of race or kind or class,
And many specimens belong to each.
For think of living things:—
The race of roving beasts that roam the hills
The stock of human kind,
The voiceless herds of scaly fish
And every wingéd thing,
All these are born as specimens, each of a class.
And so you must confess
That sky and earth and sun and all that comes to be
Are not unique but rather countless examples of a class.
For these are, too, of mortal body born,
The deep-set boundary stone of life awaits these too,
As much as every human body here on earth,
As much as every class of things,
Abounding in examples, kind by kind.

We see Nature, in freedom now, her tyrant lords dethroned,
accomplish everything—without the help of gods

AND if you learn this lesson well and cling to it
Why then you'll see
Nature in freedom now, her tyrant lords dethroned
Accomplish everything by her own spontaneous activity,
Without the help of gods.
For who by holy heart of gods
(Of gods who in their tranquil peace pass placid years,
A life of calm)
Who can prevail to rule the mighty sum of infinite universe
To guide the deep, to hold in mighty hands the reins,
To turn around the many firmaments at once,
To warm the fruitful lands with heaven's fires,
Be omnipresent everywhere,
To darken sky with clouds,
And shake the calm expanse of sky with thunderclaps,
And shoot the thunderbolts,
And sometimes wreck the temples of the gods themselves,
Or rage with might and main through solitary wilderness
And hurl the bolt of wrath which often spares the impious
And does the innocent to death?
And since the morning of creation for the universe—
The natal day of sea and earth,
The primal rising of the sun,
A multitude of atoms have been added to the universe,
Atoms flowed in from every side
And these the mighty total of the universal power
Has tossed around and brought to union,
That out of these the mighty spaces of the sky might gain fresh
room,
To raise its lofty vault to loftier heights,
Far from the earth, letting the air mount up.

FOR, from all sides, atomic bodies are distributed by blows
Each to its own, each passing to its kind—
Moisture to moisture, earth increased by earth,
Fire forges fire, sky fashions sky,
Till Nature the universal Mother of the universe
With fashioning, perfecting hand
Brings them to final end, the end of growth.
This end arrives
When nothing more is given to the veins of life
Than what flows out and ebbs away.
At this point growth of everything must stop
And Nature by her mighty power prevents increase.
For when you see a thing grow large with merry growth
And rung by rung ascend the ladder of maturity
You know that then the thing is taking more into its frame
Than it sends out—
(So long as food is passed within the veins quite easily,
So long as body is compact, the thing does not expend
More than it needs to grow.)
Now raise both hands and yield,
Admit that bodies flow from things and leave;
That even more accrue
Until the things achieve the pinnacle of growth.
And after that
Time bit by bit breaks down their strength,
Grinds down their ripened power,
To make it worse.
The larger is the thing, the more endowed with size,
When time arrives that it disintegrate
The more it scatters atoms every side at once.
It's harder for the food to seep through all its veins.
Nor is there matter in the universe enough

To rise, and keep supplied the mighty mass
And compensate for seething bulk of atom stuff
Which such a mighty mass gives out.
And so it's not unreasonable
That mighty things like this should die,
When ebbing of the atom tide makes scant the atom store,
That things like this, however great, should die and yield before
external blows,
When at the end nurture neglects the agéd life
While bodies from without pound ceaselessly
And wear it down and break its strength with blows implacable.

The universe, too, is subject to the law of growth and decay

AND so some day,
The mighty ramparts of the mighty universe
Ringed round with hostile force,
Will yield and face decay and come to crumbling ruin.
For food it is which must repair all things,
Support, renew, sustain them.
Yet in the long run all in vain.
Since when old age has come
The veins cannot receive sufficient sustenance
Nor Mother Nature give what agéd creatures need.
And even now this earth of ours is old, effete.
Scarce can it now create the tiniest animals
Though once it could bring forth the various tribes,
And bring to birth huge bodies of wild beasts.
No golden rope it was, I think, which lowered down
The various tribes of living things from sky to fields
Nor did the sea
Or waves that lash the rocks bring them to birth.
Rather the self same earth conceived and bare—
The earth which now gives living creatures sustenance

From substance of herself.
This same creative earth herself, spontaneously
First gave to mortals shining crops, the gleeful vine,
This same creative earth brought forth sweet fruits
And joyous pastures—food for grazing herds.
And these, though aided by our toil,
Can scarce grow great.
We wear the strength of oxen down, exhaust our husbandmen;
The iron ploughshare scarce suffices for our fields,
So grudgingly the land produces crops,
Seems to increase our toil.
The agéd ploughman shakes his head and sighs,
Complaining that the labour of his hands has gone for naught;
Again, again this agéd husbandman
Compares the present with the past,
Envies the fortune of his sires.
The gloomy planter of the worn-out, shrivelled vine
Bewails the times, assails the modern trend,
Curses his fate,
Recalls how ancestors, replete with piety
Supported life with ease on any narrow, tiny plot.
(In ancient times a small allotment was assigned to every member
of the clan.)
The general law our peasant fails to grasp—
That things must waste away by imperceptible degrees,
Pass to the grave,
Vanquished by time and life's allotted span.

Book Three

In praise of Epicurus, 'the teacher whom he held divine'

INTO THICK darkness came of old bright light.
  You do I follow, you, who brought the light
To show us what is good and bad in human life,
You do I follow, glory of the Grecian race,
And in your footsteps firmly plant my own.
Not that I want to rival you; affection makes me want to imitate.
How can a swallow vie with swans
Or kids with little tottering limbs
On race track vie with mighty practiced horse?
You are the father of my mind, discoverer of Nature.
From your books, O seer renowned,
You give a father's precepts in philosophy.
As bees in blooming meadows suck each flower,
So we your golden words repeatedly
We feed on them and find them golden,
Worthy of eternal life.
Soon as your thought, born of a godlike mind,
Began to thunder forth on Nature's laws,
Then all terrors from our spirit flee;
The ramparts of the world are torn apart.
I see the atoms' pageant streaming through the void.
The power of godhead is revealed,
The quiet untroubled haunts of deity,

94

Which are not shaken by the wanton winds,
Nor lashed from cloud with rain.
No snow falls white nor frost assails;
Cloudless the air that covers them, and heaven bounteously smiles,
While sky is bathed in light.
Nature supplies them all they need for tranquil life
And nothing ever mars 'their sacred everlasting calm.'
Guided by you we never catch a glimpse of Hell's recess.
Earth cannot block our vision. We can see
Whate'er goes on in space beneath our feet.
And so, thinking your thoughts
And with your guidance mastering science
A kind of godlike pleasure comes on me,
Pleasure and horror mixed,
Because your power of mind
Has left the works of Nature naked to my view.

> *'Now I must tear up by the roots and cast away
> that fear of death'*

Now since I have discoursed on atoms and have shown
What kind they are, how different in shape,
And how, self-moved, they ever fly,
In motion everlasting e'er impelled,
And how from atoms every object can be made,
Now I must tear up by the roots and cast away
That fear of death,
That fear that sullies mortal life from end to end
And pours the murk of death on everything,
Leaves no man's pleasure pure and unalloyed.
For though men often say disease and infamy
More dreadful are than deepest depths of hell;
And though they hold that soul is blood or wind
(Whichever theory they are clinging to),

And so they claim they need not our philosophy,
Yourself can judge that this is done for pomp and arrogance
Rather than deep belief.
For these same men,
Exiled from country, banished from human sight,
Black with the blackest crimes, gnawed by a hundred cares,
Live all the same.
Wherever wretchedness and anguish places them,
They worship all the same,
Butcher their sleek black bulls and give their offerings
To guardian spirits of the dead.
Their troubles turn their mind to creed and cult.
And so it's good to watch men in adversity,
By mounting dangers pressed.
At times like these
Men pour their deepest thoughts from depth of breast.
The mask is torn away, the face remains.
Then too, the lust for power and place and wealth,
Motives which make men pass the bounds of law,
And join in crime and struggle night and day
With all their might to scale the heights of wealth,
These wounds of life are too much nurtured by the fear of death.
Men see that infamy and biting poverty
Are far removed from pleasant tranquil life,
A kind of lurking at the gate of death.
These things they want to flee, spurred by false fear.
And so in time of civil war they build their wealth.
Their lust for gold outruns all bounds.
In piling wealth they slaughter heap on slaughter.
With hardened heart they gloat when a brother dies.
A kinsman's banquet they both hate and shun.
Likewise from this same fear envy can wear them down.
This man, they see, has power,

While that one wins respect and walks in fair renown,
And I, they'll say, am doused in murk and mire.
Some die to win their statues and their fame.
And sometimes even through their fear of death
Hatred of light and life takes hold of men.
With heavy hearts they kill themselves,
Forgetting that the fear of death caused all their woes.
The fear of death makes one man sully honour,
Another crash through friendship's bonds,
Wanton, in short with every human tie.
Often have men, seeking to skirt the shoals of death
Played false to fatherland and parents, too.
Like tiny boys who tremble in the dark
And think that anything may come,
We also tremble in the light and shrink from things
That in themselves are no more terrible
That what boys fear in dreams and fancy sure to be.
And so this darkened terror of the mind must be dispelled
Not by the rays of sun or gleaming shafts of day,
But Nature's laws, by looking in her face.

Life, mind and consciousness

First then I say that mind, the thing which we call intellect
In which is placed the power to guide and counsel life
Is part of man,
No less than hand or foot or eyes
Are parts of this one single, living, breathing whole.
Now some wise men have thought
That mind's activity or consciousness
Is not allotted any fixed abode within the human frame
That rather it's the body's vital state—
That which the Greeks call harmony,
Enabling man to live life consciously

97

Though intellect's located no where in our frame.
They use, as an analogy, good health.
This marks a healthy body and yet is not a part of any healthy man.
And so, they say, the mind's activity,
Is not assigned to action of a single part.
In this they seem to me to wander far astray.
It often happens that the body visible,
The whole that's clear to see, is sick;
And yet the man feels pleasure in another hidden part.
And contrariwise,
A man may wretched be in mind, yet nonetheless
Feel pleasure through his frame.
Just as a man might feel pain in his foot
And yet perhaps the while his head detects no pain.
Too when the limbs are lulled in gentle sleep
The laden body relaxed, unconscious lies,
Another part of us can all the while
Be stirred in many ways,
Receive the varied impulses of joy, the baseless cares of heart.
Thus you may know that soul resides in human limbs—
Is not a harmony at times by body felt.
This point I'll argue first—
When many portions of our body are removed,
Life lingers all the same in members that are left.
And yet when tiny portions of the vital heat have left—
And air has left the mouth,
The life then leaves the veins, deserts the bones.
From this you know
Not every part has equal role to play,
The parts do not, all alike, support our life,
But rather some—the seeds of wind and burning heat
Ensure that life should linger in our limbs.
In human bodies then are heat and vital breath

And these desert the dying man.
And now since I've disclosed
That mind and soul are truly parts of man,
Give up the name of harmony,
Once handed down to men of music from high Helicon.
(Or perhaps these same philosophers
Have dragged the name from other source, assigned it to this thing,
Which earlier was known, but lacked a name.)
In any case they're welcome to the word.
You listen to the rest of what I have to say.

Mind and life (soul) are held in unity.
The mind is physical

Now I maintain
That mind and soul are held in unity,
Create one single entity,
But that the head and lord of total man
Is reason, which we sometimes call
The mind or intellect;
That this is placed securely in the middle regions of the breast.
Here fear and terror plunge and rear;
Around these parts the surge of joy can give delight.
This, then, is intellect or mind.
The other parts of soul, spread through the human frame,
Obey the will of mind
And move at inclination of the intellect.
The mind alone knows for itself, rejoices for itself,
When not another thing has stirred
Body or soul.
Exactly as when pain has struck the head or eyes,
Th' remainder of the body feels no pain,
So the mind itself,
Sometimes feels pain, sometimes exults in joy,

But all the rest of soul through limbs and frame
Is stirred by nothing new.
And yet when intellect is stirred by stronger fears
We see the whole soul sympathize throughout the limbs,
And all the body sweat, grow pale;
The tongue is hampered and the voice is choked,
Eyes will grow misty, ears will buzz, the limbs will fail.
Indeed we often see men faint, swoon to the ground,
Through terror of the mind.
From all of this one learns quite easily
That soul is linked in union with the mind;
When smitten by the power of mind,
It strikes the body, pushes it along.
And this same line of thought will prove that mind and soul are
                                                              bodily.

For when we see
That mind and soul propel the limbs and snatch a man from sleep
Or cause a change in countenance,
And rule and turn the total man
(And none of these results can come to be unless there's touch,
And touch can never be unless it's physical)
Allow we must that mind and soul are physical.
Then, too, the mind must suffer when the body does,
With body feel the same.
If shattering shocks of hostile sword
When driven in our frame
Exposing bones and sinews, too,
Take not a human life,
Yet faintness follows and a pleasant sinking to the ground
A turmoil of the mind which happens while the warrior
Lies on the earth;
And then again from time to time a flickering will to rise.
And so the mind is physical.

When smitten with the blows of weapons physical,
It too feels pain.

What kind of matter goes to make the mind

AND now what kind of body is this mind of ours,
From what parts formed,
My poem will tell.
Now first I say that mind is formed of texture very fine,
Of particles minute.
If you're attentive you can learn from this—
That nothing happens quite so fast
As what the mind conceives and starts to do.
The mind can stir itself more readily,
Than anything that's manifest before our eyes.
Because the mind's so quick,
It must be made of atoms very round and small,
By smallest impulse movable.
Water moves, too, and ripples at the slightest touch,
Since formed of tiniest atoms—quick to move.
But honey on the other hand is more close packed,
Its fluid sticky and its movements slow.
Its mass of matter clings together more;
Its atoms certainly are not so smooth, so fine, so round.
The tallest heap of poppy seed by lightest, gentlest breath
Will tumble down and dissipate before your eyes.
A pile of stone, a heap of grain
So slight a breath would never move.
The tinier, smoother atom forms enjoy the more mobility.
Things that are rough or heavy are more stable far.
Now since the mind enjoys supreme mobility,
Its atoms must be very small and smooth and round.
And this to know, good sir, will useful be in many ways.
You'll find it good to know.

One fact will demonstrate how fine the texture of the mind,
In what small space the mind might be contained,
If gathered in a mass.
That when the quiet peace of death has seized a man,
When mind and soul have gone their way,
No stock of matter from the body goes
That sight or weight might test.
The whole dead body lies untouched, entire;
Nothing has gone except the life—a little touch of heat.
Hence it must be that soul is made of very tiny atom seeds
Joined throughout sinews, flesh and veins.
And when it's gone
The contour of the limbs is left unchanged,
No weight is lost.
Just as when bouquet from a splendid wine has passed away,
Or lovely breath of perfume scattered through the air,
Or taste has gone from any food;
And yet no one of these seems smaller to the eyes,
No weight seems lost.
For many tiny atoms go to make the taste or scent of things.
And so once and again you know,
That intellect and soul are made of atoms very small
And when they go no weight seems to depart.
But this we must not think—
That mind and soul are single in their substances.
Thin air departs from dying limbs, mingled with heat;
And heat draws air with it.
(No heat there is that is not mixed with air.)
For heat is rare and many atoms of the air must move in it.
So now we've seen that soul's of three-fold nature made.
And yet these three are not enough to bring forth consciousness.
Our mind cannot admit that any of the three
Can stir the motions that bring consciousness

The thoughts that intellect revolves.
And so we must assume another principle—a fourth;
Now this completely lacks a name.
Than this
Nothing could be more mobile or more fine,
Of smaller, smoother atoms made.
And it first sends abroad
The movements that bring consciousness throughout the limbs.
For it's stirred first since made of tiniest atom shapes.
Then heat receives the motions, and the hidden power of wind
And then the air.
And so the whole is moved.
Blood is whipped up, the whole flesh thrills,
And last of all it reaches marrow and the bones
Whether it's pleasure that stirs,
Whether emotion of a different kind.
But pain cannot assail the marrow or the bones,
Or serious illness without a dire result,
Without a perturbation of the whole,
Until no place is left for life,
Until the parts of soul scatter and leave,
Through all the body's pores.
But to these movements generally, limit is set,
As if the surface of the body kept them checked.
And so we're strong to keep our life.

How the four parts of life and mind are linked

AND now I have a deep desire to tell
In what way these four parts are linked
And how combined that they can act.
Against my will the poverty of Latin speech prevents.
Yet touch the theme I will though hastily.

103

For atoms course about among themselves,
Their motions intertwined.
So none of these four elements from the others can be separate
Nor function if there's space between it and the rest.
Though several forces they inhere
And form one substance as it were.
Just as in the flesh of every living thing
There's smell and heat and taste,
And yet these form the single growth that makes the living thing
So heat and air and hidden wind together mixed
With that one nameless, mobile force
To make one unity;
This gives the start of motion from itself
And thus the movements that bring consciousness arise throughout
the flesh.

Now this fourth principle lies deep within.
Within our body nothing could be deeper placed;
And yet it is the very soul of soul.
For as the force of mind and power of soul
Is to our members and our total frame—
Mingled in secrecy because composed
Of atoms few and rare
So in our soul, this nameless element,
Of tiniest particles composed
Is hidden, forms the very soul of soul,
And in the total body holds its sway.
In just this way and by a law inexorable,
The air and wind and heat must mingle through the limbs,
Exert their powers;
(Though one may be above, below the rest,
Be more or less conspicuous),
That single entity be seen composed from all,

Lest heat and wind apart, the power of air apart,
Should put an end to consciousness
And by their dissolution break it up.
And too the mind possesses heat—
The heat which mind assumes when tempers blaze,
When fire is seen to flash from savage eyes.
And too, the mind possesses much cold air—
The cold which goes along as fear's companion,
To start a shudder in the limbs, to stir the human frame.
And peaceful air it has,
When breast is tranquil, face is calm.
But animals possess a greater share of heat,
Creatures whose fiery heart and mind irascible,
Flames easily in rage.
To illustrate I mention first the violent rage of lions.
These often groan, their breasts break out with mighty roar,
Their hearts cannot contain the seething billows of their rage.
The chilly minds of deer have more of wind.—
This rouses more swiftly the frigid breath throughout their flesh,
Which makes a tremble run through all their limbs.
But cows live more with quiet air,
The smoking torch of wrath is never set to it—
To rouse it overmuch and spread within
The shadow of a murky mist,
Nor is it pierced and chilled with frigid shafts of fear.
The cow is placed midway between the deer and raging lion.
And so it is with men,
Though culture might polish two men's surface equally,
Those primal traces of the nature of the mind,
It leaves in each.
Nor can we think it possible
To tear up by the roots and cast away those evil impulses.
For one will swifter fall to bitter rage,

Another be assailed by fear,
A third will view things placidly, more than he should.
And by necessity in many other ways
The diverse natures of mankind, the habits that accompany them
Must differently emerge.
The secret cause of all these differences I cannot now disclose—
Discover names for all the varying atom shapes
Whence this variety arose.
One thing I see and can affirm.
So slight the traces of these evil impulses
Which reason could not drive away for us
That nothing prevents mankind from making for himself a life,
Quite worthy of immortal gods.
And so this soul is guarded by the body as a whole
And guards the body in its turn.
It is the cause of life.
The two entwine and cling with common roots.
To tear the two apart would mean destruction for the whole.
You cannot tear the scent from lumps of frankincense
Without destroying it.
And so it is with body and with soul.
They're born with atoms closely intertwined,
Endowed with common life.
Nor, as is clear to see,
Can mind and body feel apart, have consciousness,
Either of these alone without the other's force,
But by the common motions of the two,
Our consciousness is kindled, blazes strong throughout the flesh.
Then too, the body is not born alone, nor grows alone,
Nor can it last when dead.
Water can often give up heat,
The heat assigned to it;
And yet the water is not torn apart, remains unharmed.

The abandoned corpse cannot, like water,
Bear this breaking up, this dissolution of the soul,
But dies, is torn asunder, rots apart.
So from the start of life, even while hidden in the mother's womb,
Body and soul in mutual union
Must learn the movements that give life,
Nor can they divide
Without corruption, rot, decay.
So you may see,
That as the cause of life is linked in unity,
So must the substances of soul and body link themselves in one.
Now for the rest,

Feeling and consciousness

IF any person hold that body does not feel,
But soul, commingled through the frame,
Takes up the motion—the movement we call consciousness
He takes his stand 'gainst matters evident and true.
But when the soul has passed away, some one may say,
The body too is quite bereft of consciousness.
Yes, for the body loses what was not its own in life.
And many other things it loses too,
When driven from its life.
And then, to say that eyes see nothing of themselves,
But soul peeps out through eyes like opened doors—
That's hard.
The very sense experience of the eyes
Leads to an opposite result.
The life of sense itself must drive us, hurry us
To eyes themselves.
Especially when we often fail to see some gleaming thing
Because the light of eyes is blocked by light itself.
Doors don't behave this way.

The doors through which we see do not feel pain
When opened wide.
Moreover if our eyes were doors
The mind could better see were these removed—door posts and all.

Refutation of Democritus

IN all this argument about the sense
There's one point now which you must not accept
Although the judgment of that splendid, holy man, Democritus
Presents it for our thought.
The atoms of the body and the soul, he held, must alternate—
Set side by side—first body and then soul;
And placed like this they weave
The web of human limbs.
In opposition to Democritus my view is this;
Atomic particles out of which our soul is made
Are smaller far than those which make the body and the flesh.
They're fewer too, and sparsely scattered through the frame.
Thus you can promise this:
The primal atoms of the soul maintain between themselves
Spaces as great as is the size of bodies thrown at us—
Bodies, I mean, which of themselves awake,
When thrown at us, the movements that bring consciousness within
the soul.

The body does not feel without an impulse of the mind

FOR sometimes we are not aware
That dust has settled on the surface of our frame,
That dust of chalk is clinging to our limbs;
We do not sense the mist by night,
Or thin fine filament of spider's web that nets us in our walks;
We do not know its filmy mesh has fallen on our heads;

Feathers of birds we do not feel or flying thistle down;
These things exceeding light yet drift exceeding slow.
The reptile passage of a crawling thing
We scarcely feel, nor every individual print of tiny feet
Which gnats or other insects plant upon our frame.
So many things must first be stirred in us
Before the atoms of our soul, diffused throughout the structure bodily
Can feel the atoms of the body struck,
Before they can,
By jostling in the spaces set between
Rush into unity, unite and jump away in turn.
Mind is the guardian of the fortress of our life,
More sovereign for our life than power of soul.
Without the mind and intellect no part of soul
Survives throughout the limbs for tiniest space of time,
But, like attendant slave, mind follows easily
But scatters in thin air and leaves the frigid limbs in death's cold chill.
But he whose mind and intellect have firm abode
Remains alive.
Though trunk be mangled, limbs hewn all around,
The man lives on, draws in life's vital airs.
Deprived, if not of all, yet greater part of soul,
A man survives, still clings to life.
If an eye is mangled all around
Yet the pupil still abides unharmed,
The vital power of sight stands firm.
(Of course you must not cut the eyeball all around
Leave th' pupil standing by itself;
If you did this, you'd kill them both at once.)
But if that tiniest centre of the eye should be destroyed,
Then sight dies too and darkness deep descends,
Although the shining orb is otherwise unharmed.
In compact strict like this are soul and mind together bound.

That mind and tenuous soul,
in living things were born, that die they must

AND now that you may learn that mind and tenuous soul
In living things were born, that die they must,
I will unfold before your eyes,
My deepest thoughts, investigated long,
The product of sweet toil and worthy of your deepest thought.
Your task it is with strength of mind's imagining
To hold both mind and soul, in thought, under one name.
Then when, for purpose of my exposition,
I speak of soul, and prove that it must die,
Think that I speak of mind as well,
Since these are bound in one, and form one entity.
First then,
Since I have shown that soul is made of tiny things
And atoms smaller far
Than liquid wet of water, or than cloud, or smoke,
In speed the soul surpasses them and moves more easily,
When smitten by the slightest force.
For soul is stirred by images of lightest things, of smoke and cloud.
For often when we're deep in sleep
We see the altars of the gods breathe smoke, send steam on high,
And these without a doubt are images.
And now when jars are smashed,
You see the liquid trickling out on every side,
The water forming streams, this side and that.
And cloud and smoke you see dissolve in air.
And so you must believe
That soul is scattered too and faster vanishes,
Is faster sundered into atom forms,
When once it leaves man's limbs and goes its way.
And since the body
Which for soul is, as it were, containing vase or vessel,

When once it's smashed, worn thin,
Cannot contain the soul,
When once the blood has left the veins,
How could a man maintain that air contains the soul,
When air is porous, in a way that human body cannot ever be?

Mind and body are born together, grow together and die together

THEN, too, we know that intellect
Is with the body born, with it matures, grows old.
The judgment of a babe is always weak,
As is his body with its tiny tottering limbs.
But when the span of years has brought maturity and ripened strength
Wisdom grows too, the power of mind grows strong.
But then again,
When body by the savage strength of time is smashed,
And all the limbs are wasting with a blunted force,
Then reason also limps, the tongue at random strays,
The power of intellect goes stumbling,
The whole man fails at once.
And so it's natural
That soul in every part should be dissolved,
Like smoke when borne on breezes of the air.
For as we see
Soul is with the body born
And grows with it,
And then in time and step by step,
Grows faint and old and worn.
Another point is here that we can see.
As body's self must be a prey to fell disease and pang of pain,
So must the mind endure sharp care and grief and fear.
So it's not strange that mind should share in death.
Often in sickness that seems at first sight bodily,
The mind too wanders far astray;

III

It loses sanity and utters language in delirium,
And often in a grievous lethargy
The mind is carried off to deep unending sleep,
While eyes are heavy, cranium nods.
And mind hears not the voice, knows not the face
Of those who stand around and call it back to life,
The while they wet the face and cheeks with floods of tears.
And so you must admit
That mind, too, is dissolved,
When touch of fell disease has entered it.
For pain and sickness both are carpenters of death
A thing we've come to know by thinking on the death of many a man.
Nay more when piercing strength of wine has entered a man's heart
Why must there follow then a heavy feeling in his limbs,
Why must his legs be tangled up in staggering walk?
His tongue grow thick, the intellect grow soaked,
While tears swim in his eyes and shouts and sobs and oaths abound?
And all the other symptoms of a man who's drunk?
Why but that violent power of wine
Confounds the soul within the body hid?
But what can be bemused and tripped will demonstrate,
That if a stronger force has made its way within,
The thing must perish utterly, be robbed of further life.
Then, too, a man may be a prey to fits,
Before our very eyes may be a victim of the seizure of the dread dis-
ease

And falls as though by lightning stroke,
While foam comes oozing from his lips,
His body's seized with groans and shivering,
His mind grows blank, muscles grow taut,
He writhes and gasps, and, tossing to and fro,
Wearies his limbs.
His soul throughout his body, torn by the dread disease

Boils up and sends forth foam;
Just as on salty sea the waters churn
Swept by the blast and sturdy strength of violent winds.
Then from the victim of the fit a groan is wrung,
Because, you know, his limbs are racked with pain;
And more because atomic particles of voice
Are driven out from him, in dense array are carried from his lips,
Along their accustomed way, along their pavéd path (to use a meta-
                                                            phor)
And madness follows, as the power of mind and soul is torn apart,
Is rent and torn and tossed, this way and that,
And pulled to bits by this same poison's power.
But then, when causes for the malady have ebbed,
And when the sickly body's blackened bile
Has sought again its hiding place,
He staggers, as it were, and tries to rise;
And bit by bit his consciousness returns, his soul's regained.
Since mind and soul are tossed by gusty waves of malady,
And wretchedly are rent asunder and distressed,
While still by body pent,
How could you believe,
Outside the body in the open air,
They could survive and live their life,
While battling with the stormy winds?
Then, too, we see that mind can in itself be healed,
Just like a body pressed by maladies,
That mind can be improved by medicines.
This, too, will warn us that the mind has mortal life.
If one attempt to change the structure of the mind,
Or any other natural thing,
This he must do by adding here and there a bit,
Or taking some away,
Or changing the arrangement of its parts.

A thing immortal cannot be so changed—
You cannot add to it, subtract or interchange its parts.
But what is changed, beyond its limit goes,
This is the death of that which went before.
So, if the mind is sick, it shows, as I have proved,
That it was made a mortal thing;
If, equally, by healing arts it's cured,
This proves the same.
And thus the truth and fact refute opinions false;
And shut off refuge if one wants to flee,
Put, like a two-edged sword,
Erroneous views to rout.
Again we often see a man die bit by bit—
As limb by limb he loses living consciousness.
And first the toes and nails grow black,
Then legs and feet must die,
The footsteps of cold death must step by step
Creep through the frame. And as the soul is broken up and dies,
It does not issue from the structure bodily
All in one piece and in a second's time;
We have to think it's overwhelmed by death.
Now if perchance you think that soul alone
By its power contracts itself within the human frame
Collects its parts and groups them in one place,
And so withdraws sensation from the limbs;
If this were so it certainly must be,
The part where soul collects must have a greater share of conscious-
ness,
Perception more intense.
But since a place like this cannot be found,
You must believe, as I have said before,
That soul is torn to bits, disintegrates,
And, therefore, dies.

But even if, for sake of argument,
We were to grant a moment what is false,
Allow a moment that it's possible
That when a man by stages leaves this life,
As limb by limb the soul ebbs out,
His soul could be collected in one part,
Yet still we must confess the soul's mortality.
It matters not at all whether it dies
And scatters through the breezes of the air,
Or shrinks into itself from all its parts,
And so grows dull and brutish;
Since consciousness must more and more leave all the man
And less and less of life remain in every part.
And since the intellect is just a single part of man,
In certain parts is fixed and has its seat—
Like eyes and ears and all the organs of the sense which govern life—
And just as hands and eyes and nose,
When sundered from the body, cannot feel or be;
But rather in a tiny interval of time
Must know corruption;
So mind cannot exist without the man, without his frame corporeal,
The man, who seems to be the vase containing mind,
Or any other image you might choose to use,
Since body clings to mind with binding ties.
Then, too, the lively powers of body and of mind,
Find strength in mutual unity and so enjoy their life.
For mind alone, without the body's help,
Cannot produce the movements that give life,
Nor yet, without the soul;
Can body live, feel consciousness.
Just as we know the eye itself,
If torn out by the roots
Can never see without the body's help,

Just so the mind and soul without the body's help,
Are powerless.
In closest union mingling through the veins and flesh,
Through bones and nerves,
The atoms of the two are tightly held by all the frame;
They cannot leap about through mighty intervals.
And so, confined within the body's prison cell,
They start the movements which give consciousness.
But after death, outside the frame, exposed to airy breezes of the sky,
These movements soul can never start,
Because it's not contained in anything.
For we should have to think that air were pulsing life,
If in the air the soul can keep its self-identity;
Confine itself to those same motions which bring consciousness,
That while it lived it could create
In body and in nerves.
And so I say again,
When once enfolding body has been smashed,
When once the breath of life is driven outside,
You must admit
That consciousness of mind and soul have been undone,
Since cause of life for both lies in their close knit unity.
Again,
Since body cannot bear the dissolution of the soul,
Without decay and stench,
How can you doubt that soul has risen up from deep within,
And trickled out, dissolved like smoke in air?
How can you doubt that body, too, has changed,
Has fallen crumbling in a mighty ruin,
Because its footings have been shaken from their place,
When soul went trickling from the limbs,
Through all the winding ways which find themselves,
In body and its pores?

And thus you learn in many ways,
That soul was scattered through the frame and left the limbs;
Before it slipped away and swam upon the breezes of the air.
And even while it moves within the boundary stones of life,
Yet often from some cause the soul is seen
Shaken and moved and panting for release from all the body's bonds.
The face grows pale as in the hour of death,
And all the limbs grow limp on bloodless trunk,
It's just as when we say of one
'His mind is gone' or then again,
'He's fainted dead away.'
Confusion reigns and all his friends
Strive to hold fast his last frail link with life.
For then the intellect is shaken through and through
And all the power of soul,
And both collapse,
Yes and the body, too.
A little stronger blow would bring him death.
Why do you doubt that soul, so frail a thing it is,
If from the body driven out,
In open air at last, its shelter lost,
Could not endure through endless time,
Could not endure the twinkling of an eye?
For any man at point of death can never feel,
Uninjured spirit leaving from the frame entire,
Nor rising to the throat, nor reaching first the jaws,
But rather as a whole,
It dies in all the parts of body to which it was assigned,
Just as he feels that other senses fail—
Each in its place.
But soul if deathless would not so lament as now it does,
At facing death;
Rather rejoice that nows the chance to go,

And leave behind its frame outworn
Just as a snake leaves skin behind.
And now,
Why does not intellect, the judgment of the mind
Arise in head or hands or feet?
Rather for every man it comes
In single seats and fixed abodes.
Surely that certain parts assigned to each are fixed,
And here each faculty is born and here it dwells.
And here with many parts arranged and fixed it stays,
That never can the order of its limbs and parts
Be scrambled, disarranged.
So surely thing must follow thing;
Flame is not born from flowing streams,
Nor cold from fire.

The soul has no consciousness apart from the body

AND now, if soul were really deathless and could feel
When left alone, outside the body's frame,
We must, I think, imagine soul endowed with senses five.
For this we must assume to picture to ourselves
The disembodied spirits wandering through Acheron.
And so the writers of an earlier day,
The painters of the past have pictured them.
And yet not eyes, not hand, not even nose,
Nor tongue nor ears,
Apart from body can the soul possess.
Without the body, therefore, soul can never feel, nor even be.

Soul or life pervades the whole body

AND since we see that consciousness of soul,
Pervades the total frame,
And since the total body is a living thing;

If some power of a sudden cut the body into two,
With swiftest force,
And leave the segments severed each from each,
Without a doubt the soul will equally be cleft in two,
Be torn asunder, severed as the body is.
But—what is cut and severed into parts,
Without a doubt gives up its claim to immortality.
Men tell how battle chariots with scythes attached to wheels,
Hot in the wild confusion of a fight,
Can cut the limbs from off a man so suddenly,
That severed limb is seen to shiver on the ground;
And yet the power and intellect of man
Cannot feel pain, so sudden was the stroke,
So full his mind absorbed with frenzy of the fight.
With all the body that is left he presses to the fray,
And often fails to know
That arm and shield alike have gone,
Dragged by the wheels,
And rolled around by horses' hooves and ravening scythes.
Another fails to see
His strong right arm has gone,
The while he climbs and presses on.
And yet again a man may strive to rise
Though leg is lost,
And at his side and on the ground
The severed, dying foot
Twitches its toes.
Yes,
And even head lopped off from warm and living trunk
Keeps yet the look of life and opened eyes,
Until the last faint vestiges of soul have gone.
So then if impulse comes to you,

To chop to bits a snake—its quivering tongue and threatening tail,
Then all the parts you'll see writhe from the recent blow,
Cover the ground with blood;
While serpent's head with open mouth
Makes for the tail,
To still by biting it the burning pain,
That sets in from the wound.
Are we to hold that soul resides in all these little parts?
And if we do,
Then every living thing must own
Multiple souls.
And thus that living entity, immortal soul,
Once thought a unity,
Is with the body hacked to bits.
So, body and soul alike are subject to mortality,
Since each alike is cut in many parts.
Then too,
If soul has lived from endless time,
And enters in the body at its birth,
Why is that we can't recall the time that's passed,
Why not preserve a trace of what has gone before?
For if the power of mind is so much changed,
To have no recollection of the past,
That state I think is very close to death.
If it were true that living power of mind
Were wont to enter in our structure bodily,
Just when we're born and cross the threshold into life
It would not make sense that soul should grow as body grows
Grow with the limbs and in the very blood.
Rather the soul would by itself abide alone,
Cooped like wild beast within some hollow cage,
But yet in such a way that body as a whole
Could teem with consciousness.

And so again, again I say,
We must not think that souls can be released from laws of birth
                                                    and death.
Nor could we think them closely with the body linked
If souls were grafted in the body from outside.
But very fact declares the truth of this close union;
For soul is interlaced through veins and flesh and nerves and bones,
So much that even teeth can have their share of consciousness;
Pain strikes the teeth,—a twinge from water cold,
A pang if one should bite a little stone
Concealed within a piece of bread.
So closely intertwined they are,
That souls can never issue forth entire,
Resolve themselves intact from sinews, bones and joints.
But if by chance you think,
That soul is grafted in us from without,
And then floods all the limbs,
In any case so much the more you're bound to think,
That soul must perish when it's poured abroad
From body's guardian shrine.
For that which permeates, dissolves—
And so must pass away.
For soul is parcelled out through all the body's pores;
Just as when food, when spread through all the human limbs,
Must die, create new substance from itself,
So soul and mind, even though they entered whole
In body newly born,
Must as they permeate, dissolve.
And so we see
That soul and life lack not their birthday hour,
Nor funeral chant of death.
Next point,
Are seeds of soul left in the lifeless clay,

Or are they not?
If they were left behind and linger there
We cannot rightly think the soul endowed with immortality.
You see it left the body crippled and maimed,
Since part of it remained behind.
But if soul left and fled with all its parts intact
And left no part of soul within the corpse,
How is that the lifeless flesh
When first decay begins,
Begins to teem with worms,
And creatures living without bones or blood,
Crawl on the heaving, bloated frame.
Suppose you think,
That souls crawl from outside into the worms
And bits of soul can enter every worm,
And do not ask why many myriad souls come back,
Where only one had left,
Still this you must ask, decide:—
Do all these souls go hunting after seeds of little worms,
Make the worms grow to have a house in which to hide,
Or are they grafted into worms full-grown?
Why should they take such pains,
To fashion bodies for themselves?
Without a body souls need never flit about,
Hungry and cold and ill.
These ills afflict the body more,
And since the soul is with the body joined,
It sometimes suffers too.
Yet grant the usefulness for them
To fashion body for themselves to dwell,
No way they could.
Souls do not fashion for themselves,
Bodies and limbs.

Nor can they graft themselves in bodies ready-made.
They cannot weave a unity so subtle, so close-knit,
Nor from experience shared,
Could mutual contacts rise.

The creature's temperament grows as the body grows, dies as the body dies

Now why does violent savagery always attend the fierce breed of lions,
Cunning the fox?
And panic flight is handed down to deer as patrimony from their sires.
The father's fear seems to excite their limbs.
And other habits of this kind are handed down,
Implanted in the spirit and the limbs from dawn of life.
It must be that a certain temper of the mind,
Determined by its seed and breed,
Must grow as body grows
In every race of living things.
Were soul immortal and could soul exchange
Its bodily abode, then we should find
Some living creatures with mixed characters.
The valiant breed of dogs that's nurtured at Hyrcania
Would often flee the onset of the hornéd stag.
And hawks would flee in terror through the breezes of the air
At onslaught of the dove.
And reason would desert the human race,
Endow with wisdom the fierce, wild tribes of beasts.
Now those who follow in the footsteps of Pythagoras
Are clearly wrong, are led astray by faulty reasoning;
These say that soul immortal has to change
When it exchanges its abode, its body physical.
That which is changed dissolves, and so must die.
The parts you see, are changed
Are shifted from their earlier pattern of arrangement orderly.

Follow it must,
That parts can be dissolved throughout the limbs,
And in the end must die together with the human frame.
And even if they say
That human souls must always pass to human frames
Still I must ask,
How can a soul be foolish after being wise,
Why common sense is not found in a child,
Why foal of mare is never so well trained
As strength of mighty horse.
They must admit that in a body weak the soul is weak.
If that is so, this new admission must be also made,
That soul must be a prey to death,
It's felt a basic change throughout our limbs,
It's lost the life that once it knew, its earlier consciousness.
How could the power of mind be strong enough
To wax and grow, attain the longed for bloom of life,
Unless it join the body at its earliest birth?
Why does it want to leave the agéd limbs and go outdoors?
Is it afraid to stay within the palace of decay,
Afraid its home, worn by the weight of years,
Might topple on its head?
Immortal things should know no risks.
Again to think that souls throng round in idleness
When humans mate, creatures are born;
In countless numbers souls immortal wait for mortal limbs,
That souls should wrangle,
Fight to get first chance,
All this is foolishness, my friend.
Unless perhaps you think,
That souls have made a compact in advance
Agreed that that which first comes winging on its way
Have prior choice; and thus avoid a fight.

We surely cannot think that mind and consciousness
Are linked with every object bodily;
Trees cannot live in air, nor clouds in salty sea,
Nor fish in fields, nor blood in logs, nor sap in stones.
Fixed law ordains where each thing live and grow.

So mind can never be without the brain

So mind can never be without the brain,
No consciousness apart from blood and cells.
For if it could it's far more plausible
That mind should lurk in head and shoulders,
Even in the heels or any other part of man.
At least the human vase remains the same.
But since, even within our human frame,
There is a law, a fixed determination,
Where mind and soul can live apart and grow,
We must the more deny, that outside human frame,
The mind and soul could live and be.
And so when body dies you must confess,
That soul dies too, is torn to bits throughout the human frame.
And then to think, that they can mutually act or feel,
(Confounding mortal with immortal things)
Is foolishness.
For what can we conceive that's more at variance,
More inharmonious, more different,
Than things immortal with the mortal linked,
Abiding things with transient linked
To brave great storms of life?
If ever things can last for evermore,
It needs must be
That either they are made so solidly,
Repelling all assaults

Allowing no external force to penetrate and loose the close-locked
parts;
(Examples of this kind we've shown before.)
Or that they last throughout eternal time,
Because exempt from blows, as is the mighty void of space,
Eternally remain intact and suffer nothing from the blows.
Or else because there is no space around
To which things might withdraw,
When torn asunder and when broken up;
(Just as the total sum of things is infinite in time and never dies.)
No space where they might scatter;
No bodies, too, to fall on them and break them up with massive
blows.
But if the soul is thought immortal on account of this;
Because by force of life it's fortified;
Or things to harm its life come not at all;
Or then again,
Because if any come,
They leave us beaten and subdued,
Before we feel the hurt at all.
Plain fact can show this is not true.
Not only does the soul feel sick when body's sick,
Torments for the future soul can also feel;
Is often sick with fear, worn out with care.
And often when its evil deeds are past and done,
Sin brings remorse. There is the frenzy proper to the mind—
There is the utter plunge in waters of oblivion.

Death then is nothing, affects us not at all,
since mind is held to be of mortal stuff

DEATH then is nothing, affects us not at all,
Since soul is held to be of mortal stuff.

And just as in the past we knew no ill
When Punic hosts from all sides rushed to war,
When all the earth beneath the lofty shores of sky,
Trembled in dreadful battle,
And men could doubt which side was doomed for fall
And loss of empiry on land and sea alike;
So, when we're dead,
When soul and body out of which we're formed, one entity,
Are torn apart in death,
Nothing can touch our sense at all or move our consciousness
(For we shall not be alive to know.)
Even if ocean were with land confused and sea with sky.
Even if mind's structure and the power of soul have consciousness,
Still that can nothing mean to us,
We who're created what we are,
One creature by the wedlock and the mating of our body to our soul.
Even if time could collect again our particles of matter after death
Arrange them once again as once they were;
If it were given us to live once more,
That fact could nothing mean to us at all,
When once is burst the self-succession of our consciousness.
Even now, we care not for the "self" that once we were,
No torment for that "self" e'er touches us.
If one gives thought to time's immensity,
And atom's motions in their infinite variety,
This you could easily conceive,
That this atomic structure out of which we're made,
Might once have found before
The same exact arrangement of its parts.
But this we cannot grip at all with grasp of memory.
The pause of life has intervened;
The movements of our consciousness
Have wandered far and wide.

If pain and grief are due to touch a man
That man must live and be to feel these things.
Since death has taken this away,
Forbids the man to *be* whom pain might strike,
From this we learn there's naught to fear in death;
That once a man is dead he cannot be in misery,
That there's no difference if he never had been born,
When death immortal once has snatched away our mortal life.
So when you see a man lament
That after death his body rots away,
Is licked by flame or torn by teeth of beasts,
This you must know;
His words do not ring true,
Some hidden goad is lurking in his heart,
Even while his verbal creed denies
The fact of consciousness in death.
He does not (here's my view)
Follow his verbal creed nor ground thereof.
He does not fully tear his roots from life and throw himself away.
He unconsciously assumes a part of him remains.
For when a man, while still alive,
Pictures his body after death,
Imagines birds and beasts are gnawing at the corpse,
Indulges in self-pity,
His thought has failed to free his sense from that poor corpse,
Confounds it with himself and thinks the body "he."
And so he groans that he was born a mortal man,
And does not see that in real death there'll be no second self,
To live and mourn the dead and stand in lamentations,
While the self outstretched is torn or burned.
For if, when dead, it's evil to be torn by teeth of beasts,
Why is it not as bad to lie on scorching flames and shrivel up,
Or suffocate in honey when embalmed?

Grow stiff with cold when sleeping under weight of ponderous slab?
Or feel oppressed and ground by weight of earth above?
"No more," they say, "no more can joyful home fires welcome you,
Nor loyal comely wife,
Nor children be the first to share a father's kiss
And touch the heart in joyful well-springs of content."
"No more," they say, "can you be prosperous and guard your own."
"Poor wretch," they say, "how wretchedly
Has death's accursèd single day snatched life's best gifts."
But this they do not say "You'll want these things no more."
For were their vision clear, did words conform to it,
They'd free themselves from every pang of fear.
Just as you are when lulled to sleep,
So will you be through all unending time,
Completely free from every care and grief.
But we are inconsolable in tears
While body shrivels on the awful pyre.
And time can ne'er assuage the eternal pang of grief.
This is the question we must put to him:—
"What is so bad in this?
If mortal creature turns to rest and peace,
Why should you waste away in torments of unending grief?"
Often do men do this when banqueting
(Wine cup in hand, their brows with garlands crowned)
Propose a toast and say:
"Brief is the span of life for little men,
Soon it is past and never can you call it back again."
As though in death this were the worst of torments,
That thirst should parch our throat and scorch our palate.
As though desire for any*thing* could lurk within.
No mortal mind can long for self and life
When flesh and mind alike are deep in sleep.
And sleep, for all we care, can endless be;

No longing for ourselves can linger on.
And yet in sleep atomic movements wander through our flesh,
Not far at all from those that bring us consciousness,
When man springs up from sleep and gathers wits again.
Much less, I say, can death affect us, if there can be "less,"
Than what we know is nothing.
In death the particles, more widely spread,
Let no man wake and stand again,
When once the cold release from life has hold of him.
Another argument:
Let Nature, like a judge, find sudden utterance,
Upbraiding one of us in words like these:
"Is death so great a thing then, mortal man,
That you abandon self to sickening grief?
Why do you weep and groan at death?
If life was good for you
And all its joys have not drained off,
Like water poured in cracked receptacle,
And left untasted,
Why do you not, like guest at feast of life,
Slip peacefully away, with mind serene, poor fool,
Grasp quiet and nothingness?
But if your pleasures all have slipped away and life is burdensome,
Why add some more which in its turn will slip away
And never give you zest?
Should you rather not make an end to life and toil?
For insofar as I devise and calculate
Nothing is left of pleasure, not a thing.
The same monotonous sameness always, everywhere.
But if you're not by years weighed down,
Nor limbs worn and decayed,
Still all this yet will come to you,
Even if your span of life,

To push a boulder up a hill,
And find that always as you near the top,
The stone rolls down and seeks the level plain.
Always to feed the thankless mind and fill it with good things,
When seasons of the year return,
Present their fruits and various charms,
And yet be never sated with the fruits of life,
This, I think, is what we mean
When buxom girls pour water into cracked receptacle,
Which never can be filled.
And then they tell of Cerberus,
Of Furies in their inky Stygian pit
And Tartarus that belches horrid tides of shrivelling heat from
monstrous jaws—
Idle, foolish tales of things that don't exist,
That never could exist at all.
But here in life is punishment of evil deeds—
A monstrous punishment for monstrous crimes—
Atonement for sin,
Imprisonment, the horrid hurling from Tarpeian rock,
Blows and the hangman's hook, incarceration in the deepest dun-
geon cell,
Thumb screw and rack and noose,
The pitch that turns a victim's body into living, flaming torch.
And even if you miss all these,
Still conscience making cowards in advance,
Stabs with its goads, flogs with its whips,
Since human intellect fails to perceive,
The boundary of ills, the appointed end of punishment,
Fearing that retribution for the soul be even heavier after death.
This is the life of Hell on earth for fools.
This, too, please tell yourself from time to time;
Ancus the good is dead,

A better man than you a thousand times, you greedy fool.
And many other kings and potentates are dead,
Who once were great in power, ruled mighty folk.
And that great king who bridged the Hellespont,
And led his troops by land from side to side,
On foot, on horse, crossed salty deep, insulting Ocean's waves,
Yet he is dead. He's left the light of day
And poured his soul abroad from dying frame.
And Scipio is dead, war's thunderbolt, the scourge of Carthage.
He gave his bones to earth like any unknown tramp.
And too, the finest brains in science or in art,
Boon comrades of the Muses:
Homer himself, the peerless, sceptred, crowned,
Is laid to sleep like others.
Even Democritus, when creeping age
Warned him that mind and memory were growing dim,
Of his own will met death, gave up his life.
And Epicurus, too, is dead,
Teacher and prophet, for his life is spent.
(He topped the human race in genius,
Blotting out rivals as the rising sun dims stars.)
Do you then hesitate to die, think it unjust?
You who in life are already partly dead,
Who pass the greater part of life in sleep,
Snore on your feet and never cease to dream,
And drag around a mind drugged with dull fear,
And never know what ails you,
Oppressed on every side with many a care,
And staggering like a drunk in mind's blind blundering.
If men,
When once they feel a massive burden in their heart,
Oppressing, weighing down,
Could also know the source, the cause,

They would not live their life as now we often see men do:
Not knowing what he wants one runs from place to place
As though that way he'd lay his burden down,
He often leaves his spacious home and goes outdoors,
Because he's bored at home.
And then goes back again as suddenly, finding outdoors no good,
And then he drives his nags in headlong haste to country home,
As if to fight a fire.
But let him touch the threshold and he turns right round,
Goes back to town,
Or else devotes himself to sleep and seeks oblivion,
Or sometimes rushes back to city home to visit that again.
In this way every man is striving to avoid himself.
But no man as we know can lose himself.
This self will cling to him against his will.
Because he's sick and never grasps the cause of his disease.
But were perception clear,
Then men would quick abandon everything,
Devote themselves to physics and philosophy.
What is in question after all,
Is not one hour but all eternity,
What fate awaits man after death.
Last argument:
What is this mighty evil lust for life
That makes us pass our time in panic dread
Of dangers and of doubts.
In spite of everything
Over mortal man there always hangs
Death's strong immortal hour.
We cannot dodge at all the facts of life and death.
Always we tread the same old weary futile path,
Never escape.
Nor is new pleasure hammered out by length of days.

But while the object of our longing is away
That seems of all things best by far.
If we get that for which we yearned,
Then something else seems best.
A thirst for life unquenched
Makes thirst for life unquenchable,
Holds us with greedy, gaping mouth.
Then too,
What time's unfolding years will bring to us
Is still unclear.
What luck we'll have, how death will come.
And in the time to come
The man who died to day will not be dead a shorter time
Than he who died these many months or years ago.

Book Four

My fame is this: I touch a mighty theme,
and burst religion's bonds from human hearts

I TREAD THE TRACKLESS heights the Muses love,
  The heights not trodden earlier by foot of man.
I love to press towards unsullied rills and drink.
I love to pluck fresh flowers and weave
A splendid garland for my head.
My fame is this: I touch a mighty theme
And burst religion's bonds from human hearts.
And too, because I write on murky theme translucent verse
And coat on everything the Muse's charm.
In this I think I'm not unreasonable.
Like doctors do when they give horrid drugs to boys
First smear the glass around with honey's golden sweet;
The child's young age detecting no deceit,
Drinks goodness down in bitter guise.
He's cheated, not betrayed.
He's rather turned to health again.
Just this do I.
To some who have not tasted it, this creed of mine may seem too
                                                            grim.

Too many shrink away from it.
And so I wanted to expound for you
Deep wisdom in Pierian song,

And coat the bitter drug of reason with the Muse's charm.
In this way I might hope to hold your mind to theme both high and
hard,
Until you'd learned to master Nature's shape and form,
Learning how useful for yourself it was to make the search.
Now since I have explained to you the mind,
Out of what stuff, with body linked, it flourishes,
And how when torn apart it passes back to atom stuff.

How 'images' of things assail the mind

Now to inform you on the 'images of things'
I will begin:
A theme which touches close upon our views on mind.
These images like films, stripped from the outer shell of things,
Fly to and fro through air.
These films then strike upon the mind while we're awake,
Much more in sleep and terrify
When often we behold strange shapes
The images of those who've left the light of day,
Which often rouse us, fill us with frenzied mood
When we were lulled in sleep.
So we'll not think that souls escape from Acheron,
That ghosts can flit abroad.
Nor will we think that part of us is left when we are dead,
Body and mind alike have passed away,
And scattered into various atom forms.
And so I say, that images of things and shapes
Are given off by objects of all kinds
And leave their outer covering.
That we may learn from this however dull our wits.
Now since I have discoursed on atom shapes—
What they are like, these first forms of all things,
And how they differ in their different forms,

And how by everlasting motion stirred they ever fly;
And how each several thing is made from them,
Now I go on to treat a theme, that's very close to this—
The images of things, which we can call,
Films or even skin.
Because the image to the thing from which it's shed to wander forth
Is very like the thing, and bears the same appearance, shape and
form.

And first since objects in the cosmos visible,
Give off consistent images—
Sometimes with atoms loosely packed—
As wood gives smoke and fires give heat;
Sometimes with atoms closely packed,
As often crickets in the summer time
Put off their shapely coats;
Or calves at birth leave cauls,
Or slimy snake rubs off its vesture on the thorns,
(We often see them hanging there, these wind tossed skins.)
Since this is so
It surely proves that thin fine images are given off from outer forms
of things.

For why these emanations that I've named above
Should leave the form of things
More than the thin fine images,
Not even gaping mouth could tell.
For on the surface of a thing are many tiny atom forms
And these the object can eject in order as they stand,
And still preserve its shape—
(They're very few and all stand out on top)
For many things we often see give off these images,
Not only from the depth of self beneath,
But also from their surface, from their top.
The hue of things will serve to illustrate this point.

The awnings over mighty theatres stretched
Purple in colour, yellow, red,
Tied to the masts and beams on this side and on that,
Will flap and flutter in the wind,
And tinge the multitude assembled in the seats,
The gay scene on the stage,
The elegant array of senators—with glorious charm.
The more the doors and openings of an edifice
Are closed on every side;
The more excluded is the light of day,
The more will all things in the theatres laugh,
Reflecting a glorious sheen.
Since, then the canvas gives this hue from coloured surfaces,
So every thing gives off thin images,
In either case thrown from the top.
And so there are fixed semblances of things,
That to and fro flit round about,
Though slight in bulk and not in isolation visible.
Then too,
Odors and smoke and heat and things like these
Are given off and scatter far abroad
Because in rising, coming forth from deep within,
They tread a winding path and so are torn;
(No exits by straightforward paths there are for them
To issue as a whole.)
But when the images of colour from the surface of a thing
Are sent their way;
Nothing is there to tear it up,
Since colour in a thing is out in front and near at hand.
And then,
Whatever images appear to us mirrored in glass,
Still water, or in any other shining thing,
These too, because resembling the reflected thing

Must be composed of images of them,
And so be given off.
And so there are thin images of forms of things,
Resembling objects which they leave,
Which eye of man cannot perceive when taken one by one,
But by repeated, constant batterings they're hammered back,
And so reflect an image from the surface of the shining things.
No other way it seems could shapes so well be saved
To render images so very like originals.

How thin and fine are the images

COME now and learn how thin this image is.
And first, since atom forms are far below the grasp of sense,
Are smaller far than tiniest things that eye can not perceive;
Yet now, that I may prove this too,
Learn in few words how fine the texture of all atom shapes.
First there are tiny animalculae,
So small that just a third of them could not be seen.
What can we think their guts would be?
And what the tiny oval of the heart or eye?
What of their limbs and parts?
How tiny must they be.
What then of atom shapes from which their mind and soul must be
composed?
Do you not see how fine and how minute they are?
Some things emit a pungent odor from themselves—
The universal healing plant, foul wormwood,
Yes and the evil-smelling southern wood, and bitter centaury—
If perchance you press a specimen,
Of one of these between two fingers of the hand,
Then the scent will long remain

. . . .

Must you not rather learn that many times images of many things
Wander abroad at random, powerlessly,
Beyond the powers of human sense.

Images of clouds

Bᴜᴛ lest perchance you think
That only images from objects cast can fare abroad,
Some images there are begotten of their own accord,
Which of themselves are formed above our heads and in the vault
of sky,
Moulded in many ways they are and carried by the wind.
Often we see clouds gather in the depths of sky
And mar the still, clear visage of the universe,
And as they lightly move caress the sky.
Often the face of giants is seen to move along,
Trailing a shadow far and wide,
And sometimes mighty hills, yes and the rocks from mountains
torn,
Are seen to go ahead and move before the sun.
Sometimes a mighty beast it almost seems
Can lead and draw the clouds.
And these like fluid things never cease to change their shape,
Create the outline form of many things.
Come now I will unfold and tell,
How swiftly, easily these images are made,
To flow unceasingly from things,
And slip away and leave.
The topmost surface ever streams away from things
To be cast off.
Now when this surface reaches certain substances
It passes through—example, glass.
But when it reaches jagged rocks or wood

It's torn at once, cannot reflect the images.
But when a substance bright and dense is set across its path
As, in particular, a looking glass
Neither one of these results can then occur.
The images cannot pass as through the glass,
Nor are they torn as by the wood.
The smoothness of the glass permits them to survive.
And so the images stream back again from it to us.
And though you place the several things against the mirror suddenly
The image comes to view.
From this you know
That from the outer surfaces of things there ever flow
Thin shapes of things and fine thin images.
And so in tiniest space of time the images are born,
And rightly will you say their birth is swift.
Just as the sun shoots out so many rays of light
In shortest time,
To flood the universe with light perpetual,
Just so the many images of things
Are born in many ways, to every quarter round
And instantly, to whatsoever side we turn the looking glass,
To meet the surfaces of things
The objects are reflected back again with corresponding shape and
hue.

Then too, though sky is most serene,
A dirty storm arises suddenly,
As though on every side the murk were all poured out of Acheron,
To fill the vault of sky;
Just so when black, foul night of clouds has covered us
The dark, foul face of fear hangs overhead.
Of this how small a part an image is
There's none to tell, none can explain in words.

COME now I will proclaim in verses sweet though few
How swiftly images are carried on,
And what velocity's assigned to them,
To swim through air;
How brief the time, how long the space they cross.
Is not the shrill, brief song of dying swan
Far sweeter than the steady din of cranes
Spread through the far high clouds in southern sky?
Now first we often see
That light things made of finest atom stuff are very swift.
Example—light and heat of sun, of tiniest atoms formed
Which as it were are knocked along and never pause
In passing through the spaces of the air,
And ever by the blows behind are driven on.
In hottest haste the place of light is filled by light,
And gleam by gleam is pricked and spurred.
Now just like this the images
Can course through space unthinkable in quickest time;
A tiniest cause far off in spaces infinite
Impelled them on;
And after that they're borne along with light, swift bulk.
And then, the texture of their atom stuff is fine,
Enabling them to go through anything
And trickle through the interspace of air.
Then, too, when particles of things are given off abroad,
From deep within, like light and heat of sun,
They fall part in tiniest time,
And spread their light and heat o'er all the sky,
Fly over sea and earth and flood the firmament.
What then of things that in the forefront stand
When they're cast off and nothing hinders them to go?
Do you not see that these must further, faster move,

And course through many times the same extent of space,
In just the time that rays of sun can flood the sky?
Here's an example that will prove more clearly than the rest,
How swiftly images will leave a thing—
The moment that a pool of water, placid and still,
Is placed beneath the starry sky,
The calm and beaming stars of heaven's firmament
Are seen reflected in the still expanse.
Do you not see how instantaneously
The image runs from coasts of sky to coasts of earth?
And so again, again you must confess
With swiftness wonderful are bodies sent
To strike the vision, stir the impulses of sight.
From certain things odors pour off incessantly,
In just the way that cold pours from the streams,
Heat from the sun, spray from the Ocean's waves—
The spray that eats away the walls around the Ocean's shores.
And various voices never cease to flit through air.
Often the salty moisture fills our mouths,
When walking by the sea,
Or when we watch a dose of wormwood being mixed
Its bitter taste assails.
And so from everything must bodies flow, scatter on every side.
Nor is delay or respite granted to the stream,
Since sense is active constantly;
We never cease to see and smell and hear.

Things can be perceived by touch

THEN too, a body felt by groping hands in darkest night
Is recognized to be the same
As body seen in clear and shining light;
It follows that the sense of sight and touch are stirred
By the same cause.

145

What thing can strike our vision in the light that's cubical
Except the image of the cube.
And so I demonstrate
That cause of vision lies in images;
Without the images nothing is ever seen.
And now, what I have come to call the images of things,
Are borne from every side
Scattered abroad, distributed on every side.
But as we see them only with our eyes,
It comes to pass, whichever way we turn our sight,
That all things strike with shape and hue.
The images enable us to tell how distant is a thing from us.
For images when given off
Then drive and push the intervening air,
Glide through the eyeballs, push the pupils as it were,
And go their way.
And thus we see how distant is a thing from us.
The more of air is driven on in front of it,
The longer is the breeze that brushes through our eyes,
The greater is the distance of the thing away from us.
Of course all this occurs exceeding fast,
So that we see just what the object is, how far away.
Now this must not seem wonderful at all,
Though individual images cannot be perceived,
The object as a whole yet can.
When wind is lashing bit by bit,
Or bitter cold streams on our frame,
We do not feel each individual particle of wind or cold
But just the aggregate;
And on our body we perceive the blows
As if some thing were lashing us,
And giving us sensation of the body from without.
Then too,

If with our finger we should strike a stone
The colour and the outer surface of the stone
We touch, but do not feel.
Rather the hardness deep within is what we feel.

Reflections in the looking glass

COME now and learn
Why the reflection in the looking glass
From far beyond the surface of the looking glass is seen, seems deep
within.

It's like the images we really see through open doors
When vision is unhindered through the doors,
Lets many things outside be seen from within the house.
This sight arises from a double stream of air.
For first the air within the doors is seen,
And then the panels of the folding doors on left and right,
And then the light outside—a second stream of air brushes our eyes
And then the things we really see outside.
Just so when first the image of the looking glass is cast adrift
While coming to our eyes,
It pushes, drives before it all the intervening air,
And makes us see all this before we see the looking glass.
But when we've seen the looking glass itself,
Straightway the image borne from us,
Goes to the looking glass and is there turned back,
And drives and rolls another wave of air before itself,
And makes us see this air before we see the looking glass,
And makes it seem as far within the mirror as we stand outside.
And so we must not wonder, not at all.
(Text corrupt.)
At things which send an image back from level surface of the looking
glass;
For both of these the vision comes about from these two streams of
air.

147

And now;
The right hand members of our structure bodily
Are seen reflected in our body as the left
Because the image, striking on the level surface of the looking glass,
Is not reversed unchanged, but dashed right back;
It's just as if you hurl a plaster mask while wet
Against a pillar or a beam,
And this should keep its shape in front,
Behind should take the curving surface of the beam.*
Impressions taken from the mask would show
The eye that previously was left will now be right
What previously was right will now be left.
It often happens too,
That images by mirrors multiple are passed along,
Creating five or even six such images.
And even things concealed far back,
In deep recesses of the house
Will often send reflections to the front by mirrors multiple,
No matter how irregular the corridors.
So surely does the image pass from looking glass to looking glass
And left is changed to right and back again.
Again those little sides of mirror curved to match the human flank
Send back their images with right reflected on the right;
And this is so because the image is passed on
From part to part of curving looking glass,
And then returns to us reflected twice;

* (These) lines are extremely difficult and perhaps need further explanation. I throw a wet clay mask squarely against a post or beam, which is rounded or at any rate not flat. The front of the mask, which was roughly convex because of the features and shape of the head, bulges out backward and thus becomes concave when it hits the post. In other words, the features and contour of the mask, which originally faced the post, are protruded through the original inside of the mask and now bulge out and face away from the post. The original concave inside has now become a convex outside. Accordingly, the right eye of the mask before it struck the post is now the left eye of the reversed mask that sticks to the post and faces away from it.

SMITH-LEONARD p. 548.

Or else the image whirls itself around
When once it has arrived at surface of the looking glass
Because the curving surface teaches it to turn.
Then too you'd think that images
Walk step by step with us,
And place their feet and imitate our gait;
This is because from that part of the looking glass
Which you've just left,
No image can immediately return.
Nature compels that things be carried backwards leap by leap,
At equal angles from all other things.
And then our eyes must shun the glare of light, not look at it.
The sun can strike you blind if you should try to gaze at it.
Its power is great, its rays with power are borne
From far aloft and through the pure, clear air,
To strike the eyes and bring confusion to their parts.
Then, too, a piercing light will often blind the eyes,
It has so many seeds of fire within itself
Which penetrate and pain the sight.
Again whatever jaundiced people look upon
Becomes a sickly yellow hue
Because a yellow emanation from their frame
Flows out to meet the images of things.
And many yellow seeds are lurking in their eyes
And by their touch paint pallor everywhere.

Darkness and light

THOUGH standing in the dark we often see the things outside suf-
                                                    fused with light
Because although the nearer air, the dark air of the gloom
Has entered, seized upon our open eyes,
There follows in hot haste the light, bright air,
To cleanse the eyes and send abroad

The dun dark shadows of the earlier air.
The light is quicker far,
More powerful and more rarified.
When once it fills the passages of eyes with light,
Opened a way where once the blacker air had laid its siege,
Then images of things suffused in light can make their way,
And stimulate our pupils that they may be seen.
But on the other hand
We cannot stand in full daylight
And see the objects in the dark,
Because the darker air, the denser air, coming in last,
Fills all the passages, lays siege to all approaches to the eyes;
No images of other things can strike and stir the sight.

On illusions

Now often in the distance we perceive
The square towers of a town, which yet seem round.
The cause is this:
All angles in the distance must seem flattened out;
Or better said—
The angularity is not perceived at all;
The blow which at a closer range would strike the eye
Is dead and never strikes the battlements of sight;
The blows which journey through the distant air,
By frequent buffetings of passing wind
Are rendered blunt.
And so
When every angularity in distant objects has escaped our eyes,
The hard stone piles seem round and smooth
Like objects turned by lathes.
Though not like things which to our closer eyes are really round
They seem with outline shadowy resembling them.

Shadows

THEN, too, our shadow in the light of sun
Will often seem to move,
To follow in our steps and mock our gait.
If indeed, you choose to think,
That air bereft of light can move,
Follow the footsteps and the gait of men;
That which we call a shadow can be nothing else
Than air bereft of light.
Assuredly,
Because in certain spots in due array
The ground is cheated of the light of sun
Where we in strolling block the light of sun
But as we leave, the ground again is filled with light;
On this account it comes to pass
That what was body's shadow seems to follow still
As we proceed by straight on course.
New rays of light are ever pouring forth;
The old ones go as fast as fire burns wool.
And so, the ground is easily despoiled of light;
Is filled again with light to wash away the shadows dark.
In this we don't admit at all
That eyes are fallible.
It is the task of eyes to see the various spots of light and shade.
To reason out—whether the light's the same or not;
Whether the shade's the same, which now is here, now there—
This is the task of mind.
Eyes can never know the nature of the universe.
Do not assign to eyes the faulty reasoning of the mind.

More illusions

THE ship in which we sail is borne along,
And yet it seems quite still.

Another ship, at anchor though she rides,
Seems to be passing by.
And plains and mountains seem to fly astern
As we drive by and flit with bellied sail.
And all the stars, fixed fast in Heaven's vault,
Seem to stand still,
Though ceaselessly they move; rise and return to far off setting place,
When they've traversed all the vault of sky with bodies bright.
Sun, too, and moon seem to abide in place;
Yet simple fact reveals that these two bodies move.
And distant mountains, rising from the middle of the sea,
Seem to unite and form a single isle,
Though passage wide and free is there for ships.
When children in their games whirl ceaselessly, then stop;
They think the house is whirling, pillars racing round;
They scarce can help believe the roof is falling in.
Again when Nature in her daily course,
Begins to lift on high the sun, red with its twinkling rays—
To raise it high above the mountain tops—
Those mountain heights on top of which the sun appears to stand
And turn to red reflection of its close and glowing fire,
Those hills are scarcely distant from the place where now we stand,
Two thousand times the length of speeding arrow's flight—
Often just half a thousand times a javelin's cast;
But in between the mountains and the sun
Lie countless level leagues of sea
The ocean strewn beneath the mighty shores of sky,
And many miles of land lie in between,
Possessed by various tribes of men and various kinds of beasts.
And yet a little puddle left between the paving stones
Of city streets—
A pool no deeper than a finger's breadth
Presents a vision underneath the earth

As vast as all the huge and gaping mouth of sky above our heads.
It seems that you are looking down on clouds,
And sky,
And bodies hidden in the sky, in fashion wonderful.
And sometimes too when eager panting steed
Sticks in mid stream,
The current's force appears to take the horse along;
Though yet in truth,
Our horse is standing still,
Breasting the torrent's force,
Seeming to push the river hotly back in haste.
Where'er we turn our eyes
It seems that all things flow and rush ahead,
Just as we do ourselves.
And when we look at columns of a temples colonnade,
Although its sides are parallel,
And though the columns of support are all of equal height,
When we survey the temple as a whole from upper end,
The lines together draw, as though to pointed end of narrowing cone;
The roof is joined to meet the floor;
And left side of the building to the right;
Until the lines converge and form the apex of a cone,
And pass from sight.
To sailors tossing on the sea,
It often seems that rising sun emerges from the Ocean's waves;
And sets again in Oceans deep to hide its light.
And yet,
There's nothing they can see but sky and wave.
Thus you'll not lightly think that sense could be impugned on every
                                                    side
And found entirely fallible.
To men who're ignorant of sea,

Sea and its ways—
A ship in harbour seems to rest upon the water, fresh or salt,
Crippled and maimed with broken poop.
The portion of the oars above the salt sea spray seem straight;
Rudders seem straight;
But all the parts that pass and sink beneath the ocean wave
Seem to be broken, twisted round,
Seem to turn upwards, seem almost to float
Upon the liquid surface of the liquid sea.
And when the winds are moving scattered clouds across the sky
At dead of night,
Why then the splendid constellations seem to meet and glide
                                        athwart the clouds,
And seem to move in heaven's eminence,
On journeys different from their proper way.
Then too,
If one should chance to place a hand over one's eye and press the eye,
By some queer quirk of sight it seems
That everything is double to the view—
Double the lights of lamp with flower of flame,
Double the furnishings throughout the house
In double sets;
Double the countenance of men; their bodies double, too.
Then too,
When sleep has overcome our limbs in bondage sweet—
When all the body lies possessed by sleep profound,
Yet to ourselves we seem awake, to move our limbs;
And though the night is black we seem to see,
Sun and the light of day.
And though the four walls of the bedroom fence us in,
We seem to see new sky, new sea, new streams, new hills,
New plains we seem to traverse and to hear new sounds.
Though night's stern silence ever hems us in,

We seem to answer, seem to converse though speaking not.
And many other wonders of this sort we see;
And all of them would strive to undermine
Our confidence in power of sense.
But all in vain;
We know that most or all these sights are inference—
Added by power of mind, added by seeing self,
So that things the senses never see
Are counted, seen.

The canon of truth

THE hardest task of mind is just to separate
The open, clear and certain things,
From dubious apparitions which the mind supplies itself.
Again, suppose a thoughtful man puts up this argument:
The human mind can nothing ever know.
This judgment, too, must turn out fallible.
For he admits the limitations of the human mind;
Nothing mind can know.
With such a man I'll never join in argument.
He firmly plants his head in footprints of his foot.
And yet were I to grant that he knows this—
Namely that he knows nothing certainly,
One question I would ask:—
Since he has never yet found truth in clear perception of a thing,
How can he know what knowledge means?
What ignorance, in turn?
What then has made to grow in him
The notion of the true; the false?
And what has made him come to think
That doubtful notion differs from the sure?
But if you really face the facts of things,

This you will find:—
That the very notion of the true emerges from experience of the
sense;
That sense and sense impressions cannot be gainsaid.
For something must be found of greater certainty than sense
Which of itself can use the true to overthrow the false.
What can be found of greater certainty
Than evidence of sense?
Will power of mind, springing from sensations false,
Avail to speak against the sense,
When mind is wholly sprung from sense?
Unless the sense is true,
The power of thought and reason all is undermined.
Or could the power of ears hold court, pass judgment on the
evidence of eyes?
Or touch on evidence provided by the ears?
Will taste residing in the tongue refute the evidence of touch?
Will nose or ears expose the falsity of touch?
Not so, I think.
For of the senses each must own
Its proper power and force.
With one we know the soft, the hot, the cold,
With one the various hues of things,
And all that's linked with hue.
The taste of tongue wields its own proper power;
In one way smells arise, but sounds quite differently.
No sense can prove another false,
Nor can a sense pass judgment on itself,
Since all impressions coming from the sense
Have similar validity.
And so what they from time to time perceive
Is true.

We must not overthrow the evidence of the senses

AND if the power of mind cannot resolve the cause
Why things which close at hand seem square
Far off, seem round;
Still it is better that the poverty of reasoning
Should fail to grasp the cause of either shape
Rather than let a thing that's clearly seen
Slip from the hands;
Rather than violate man's first and basic faith
Rather than overthrow the firm and strong foundation stone
On which being and life alike must rest.
Unless you're bold to trust the evidence of sense
All reasoning will fall away;
And life itself would straightway fail,
Unless you dare to trust the sense,
Avoid the precipice of doubt,
Avoid the chasm of false reasoning
And cleave to what is sound and sure.
Hold fast to this and know it well—
That all, the arguments of sceptical philosophers
Are but an empty store of words
Set up in serried ranks against the sense.
It's just as when you start to build a lofty tower
If measuring foundations you should go astray
And if the square is not applied, or carelessly,
Or if the level sags a bit in any place,
Why then the whole great tower must go awry
Its lines will bulge and sag.
The walls will lean—backwards, forwards, out of true.
Proportions go astray;
Some parts will seem to have the will to fall,
And some will fall.
The building was betrayed by faulty judgment at the starting point.

And so your reasoning must go astray
If it arises from the false beginning of false sense.
And now I tread an easier path—less strewn with stones.

How other organs of the sense,
Perform the tasks appropriate to each. a) Hearing

I WANT to tell how other organs of the sense
Perform the tasks appropriate to each.
First then, all sounds and every voice are heard
When they have made their way into the ears,
Have struck the consciousness with impact bodily.

Voices and sound are material

THAT voice and sound are bodily, are physical,
This you must grant since they can strike the sense.
Then too, the voice can often rasp the throat,
Excessive shouting as it issues forth
Can make the windpipe rough.
In numbers great the elements of sound have risen up
Through narrow passage, when they began
To make their way outdoors.
The entrance to the mouth is rasped
When throat is choked.
No doubt can lurk then that the voice alike and words
Are made of elements bodily,
Since these can cause us pain.
You notice, too, how much of man's corporeal form
Is taken from the sinews and the very strength of human frame
By speech perpetual, speech without pause—
From gleam of rising sun until the shades of darkness fall—
The more so if one shouts.
And so the voice must be of structure physical
Since body is by frequent speech worn down.

158

Now roughness in the voice must come from roughness in its atom
                                                            particles.

And smoothness, too, from smoothness of the atom stuff.
And very different atom forms and shapes must be
When trumpet bellows deep with muffled tones
And when it's echoed back
And blares in barbarous tones with raucous buzz.
And too, when swans from winding vales of Helicon
With mournful voice raise high their shrill lament.
These voices then, when forced abroad from deep within
And shot outside straight through the lips,
The agile tongue, the skilful artifex of words
Divides and shapes them, moulds them with the lips.
And when the traversed space be not so long
Whence voice has left,
The very words are clearly heard, distinguished sound by sound.
The voice preserves its form and keeps its shape.
But if the space between be very great,
Because the voice must travel through a great expanse of air
The words must be confused;
While flying through the air the meaning's lost.
And so you hear a sound, know not the meaning of the words.
Confused and tangled comes the utterance to you.
Then too, a single word sent from the crier's throat
Will often stir the ears of all assembled in a throng.
And so one voice divides and makes quite suddenly
The force of many voices;
It strikes on many ears,
Imprints upon the words a shape and clear cut sound.
That part, however, of the utterance which falls not straight upon
                                                            the ears

Is borne abroad and dies in vain,
Diffused through space in vain.

159

And some parts beat upon the solid rock,
Are driven back, give back the sound,
And sometimes mock us with the echo of a word.

Echoes

Now when you see this well
Both to yourself and others you can well explain
How in deserted spots
The rocks give back the counterparts of words in due array
When amid darkening hills we seek our comrades lost
And call the scattered band with mighty shouts.
I myself have seen a place return
Six times or seven, the echo of a voice,
When one voice only you have sent abroad.
One hill passed on the word to neighbouring hill
And echoed what was said, time and again.
The natives think that spots like this
Are haunts of goat-foot satyrs, comely nymphs;
They say that fauns are there, whose clamour as they wander
through the night
And sportive play
Disturb the quiet silence of the placid hours.
And then are heard the strains of strings and sweet laments
That flutes pour forth, their holes by fingers stopped,
While rustic people chant.
Far over rolling country side the peasant folk
Hear sweet and piercing strains,
When Pan, the great god Pan,
Shaking the pine boughs used for covering
Half human head,
With curling lip runs over open reeds
And evermore the pipe pours out its sylvan strain.
And many other wonders of this kind they tell

That none may think these rustic folk live in a wilderness,
Places by gods abhorred.
And miracles they boast with empty words
Or spurred by hope to tell the tallest tale—
(As all the human race is over much concerned to find an audience.)

Sounds can pass where sights cannot

Now for the rest this is not wonderful,
How speech can pass through walls, assail our ears,
Where eyes can never pass to see an object clear.
We often know a conversation's going on
Though doors are closed;
Because undoubtedly the voice can pass through winding pores of
                                                            things
Where images decline to go.
For images are torn apart unless the pores are straight—
Straight like the pores of glass through which all images can pene-
                                                            trate.

Then, too a voice is broken up and spreads on every side
Since voice from other voices always springs
When once for all a single voice has issued forth
And sprung apart and formed a choir
Of many voices joined.—
Just as a spark of fire will scatter into many fires.
And so a hidden far off spot is filled with sound,
Buzzes and teems with noise.
But images must always pass by path direct and straight,
As they are once for all sent forth.
Over a wall no one can see;
But voices on the other side we all can hear.
But even the voice,
If passing through the walls and through the house,

Is blunted in its edge, enters our ears confused.
The sound we hear; cannot make out the words.

The other senses. b) Taste

THOSE organs, too, by which we sense a taste,
The tongue, I mean, the palate in the mouth,
Need not much work to tell.
First we feel taste within our mouth
When munching on our food;
We press it out as one would squeeze out water from a sponge.
What we press out is all through palate's pores distributed,
Through all the winding passages of loose-meshed tongue.
Now when the atoms of the trickling sweet are smooth
They sweetly touch and sweetly stroke
The moist and sweating vault above the tongue.
But if the thing is filled with rougher atom stuff,
So much the more it pricks the sense—attacks and tears.
Only within the limits of the palate and the mouth
Does pleasure come from taste.
When it has made its headlong way along the throat
No pleasure comes;
While food is being spread abroad through all the limbs.
It matters not what diet the body takes for nourishment,
If only you digest whate'er you take
And spread it through the limbs,
And keep the stomach uniformly moist.

Why what seems to one most sweet
seems to another evil, noisome, bad

AND now why different creatures need a different kind of food,
I will explain;
And why what seems to one most sweet,
Seems to another evil, noisome, bad.

The difference is very great.
That which is food to one to others proves
A biting poisonous curse.
There is a snake you know, which only touched with human spit,
Must straightway die, itself devour itself.
Then too the hellebore, to men a biting, poisonous curse
Makes goats and quails grow fat.
That you may learn why this is so,
This you must keep in mind—a thing we've said before—
That atom shapes are mingled in all different things,
Quite differently.
All living things that feed on food are outwardly unlike,
A different shaping of the limbs encloses them,
Kind after kind.
So they are made of varying atom shapes.
And as the atom seeds are all unlike
So are the intervals, the passages, the pores—
Different in all their limbs and in the mouth and palate too.
Some must be small, some great;
For certain creatures they must be triangular;
For others square, for many round,
For some with many angles variously arranged.
For as the motion and the shape of atom stuff demands
The passages must vary too,
Just like the texture of the stuff enclosing them.
And so, when bitter food seems sweet to some,
For him to whom the food tastes sweet,
The smoothest atom shapes
Must enter in the pores caressingly.
For him to whom it's sour
The rough and jagged atoms enter in the pores.
From this it's not so hard to judge the individual case.
When raging fever has attacked a man

Or bile flows high,
Or when the violent onset of disease is roused in other ways
Why then the body as a whole is disarranged,
And all the atom structure in the whole is disarrayed.
And what before suited his taste
Suits it no more;
But other atom shapes are better suited now
To penetrate, excite a bitter taste.
Now in the taste of honey there are mingled both—
Bitter and sweet.
And this I've often shown before.

The other senses. c) Smell

AND now I must explain
How the attack of smell can touch the nose.
First there must be many things
Of which are varying waves of scent roll on and flow.
We must suppose these waves of scent are always streaming off,
Are constantly dispatched and scattered everywhere abroad.
But various scents are fit for various creatures differently,
Because their atoms are unlike in shape.
And so the scent of honey wafted on the breeze
Will draw the bees from distant parts;
The scent of flesh will draw the carrion birds.
And then the powerful dogs sent on ahead
Guide hunting men,
Where'er the cloven hooves of fleeing beasts have turned their steps.
The bird that saved the citadel of Romulus—the white and cackling
goose—
Perceives far in advance the scent of coming men.
And so the various scents to various animals assigned
Leads each of them to find its proper food,
Makes them avoid vile poisons.

And so the various kinds of beasts are well conserved.
So thus this very scent, whatever strikes the nose,
Can be transmitted varying distances.
And yet no smell at all can go as far as sound—
(I mention not the images which strike the pupils of the eye
And stir the sight.)
For though it strays abroad,
And comes but slow and dies away too soon,
Its fragile stuff is bit by bit diffused through breezes of the air.
First because coming out from deep within the thing,
It cannot easily depart.
(That odors stream away, depart from things from deep within,
Is manifest from this—
That all things smell the more,
When broken, crushed or melted in the fire.)
Again a man must see
That smell is made from larger atom parts than voice;
It does not pass through walls,
Where voice and sound are borne—and frequently.
And so its hard to find location for the scent.
The onslaught of the smell grows cool in dallying through the air.
Nor do it's messages run hot to strike the organs of our sense.
Hence dogs must often go astray and search out footprints with their
                                                                eyes.

Not only is this true of scent and taste:
The sights of things and hues as well as scents
Are not adapted to the sense of all.
For certain creatures certain sights are much too fierce.
The cock that claps the night out with his wings,
And summons dawn with piercing cry
The ravening lions can never face or gaze upon.
They straightway think of flight.
There are assuredly in bodies of the cocks

Some certain lurking atom seeds
Which, loosed into the faces of the lions
Stab into tender pupils of the eyes
And cause sharp pain.
And this the fiercest of all beasts cannot endure.
And yet they cannot hurt the eyes of men at all.
Perhaps they do not pierce the eyes.
Or if they do
Perhaps an exit free is left for them
And so they cannot stay and hurt the eyes in any part.

'Now come, attend and learn what moves the mind'

Now come, attend and learn what moves the mind,
And whence arises that which enters into intellect;
It needs few words.
This I say first:
That many images of things are wandering on every side
In every way, in all directions bent;
And these like web of spider or the leaf of gold
Join easily.
These images are finer far
Than those which fill the eyes and stir up sight;
Since images which reach the mind
Can go through body's pores,
Stir up the unsubstantial mind and move our consciousness.
Monsters of fable we then seem to see:
Centaurs, half man, half horse;
Scylla with woman's face and breasts
Conjoined with monstrous limbs;
And Cerberus with heads of dogs and serpent's tail;
And ghosts of those whose bones the earth enfolds.
For images of every kind are flitting everywhere—
Some which are brought to earth spontaneously,

And some which leave the surfaces of things,
And some which come to be, combining various images of things.
The image of a Centaur could not come from any living thing.
Such creatures never lived.
But when fortuitously
The images of man and horse have met
They easily combine—just as we said before—
Because their nature's fine and texture rare.
And all the other monsters of mythology
Are made up so.
And since they move with lightness and mobility
As I have shown before,
In one assault these contradictory images
Can easily assail our mind.
For mind itself is fine and wondrous quick.
You yourself can learn
That this is how these combinations come to be.
Since concept of the mind is like perception of the eyes
They come to be in fashion similar.
Now since I see a lion by means of images that stir the eyes
From this we know
That mind is moved by images of lions
Or other things that mind conceives—
Just like the eyes;
Except that mind conceives the finer images.
In fashion similar,
When slumber has relaxed the limbs, the intellect keeps watch;
Except that these same images attack the mind—
The same as when we wake.
So that we seem to see a friend who's left this life,
Who's held by earth and death.
And nature makes this come to pass
Because the senses all are checked, at rest through all the limbs.

And so they cannot check the false with true.
The power of memory is also lulled to rest in sluggish sleep,
Cannot put up an argument nor prove,
That he is prey of death and doom whom intellect in dreams
Sees as alive.
Now for the rest,
There's nothing here to marvel at
That images should move and toss their limbs and arms
In rhythmic time.
In dreams we think that images do this.
For when the image passes on
And others come to take its place with posture differing
It seems as though the first has changed its gestures and its gait.
We must suppose indeed that all this happens very rapidly.
So great the speed, so great the store of things,
So great, in shortest time perceptible, the store of particles,
Whereby continuous process can always be maintained.

*If the whim takes hold of us to think of any thing
straightway our mind reflects on that same thing*

In these investigations, many questions we must ask and many things
explain,
To meet our deep desire to find the truth.
And first we ask how this can be—
That if the whim takes hold of us to think of any thing,
Straightway our mind reflects on that same thing.
Do images keep watch and ward and wait our will,
And run to fill our least behest, our slightest whim,
Whether the mood is prompting us to think
Of sea and land and sky?
And parliaments of men and pageantry—the banquet and the fight,
Does Nature for our whim create them all,
Prepare them for our mood?

(Though here and now, at this same time and place,
The folks around have minds on other things?)
And then in sleep
We see the shadowy images dancing in rhythmic step
Moving their agile limbs, shoot out their agile arms,
And then in turn the feet in harmony;
Can we suppose that images are steeped in art?
That images, with education most refined,
Go wandering in the night to tread their dance?
Would not this rather be true?
Because within a single point of time perceptible—
The uttering of a single word
Time units in a multitude unnoticed lurk,
(And this the power of reasoning perceives)
The various images are there
In various spots and in the smallest point of time.
So great the speed, so great the store of things.
For when an image flits away, another comes to birth,
Its limbs and posture differently arranged,
The former seems its gestures to have changed.
And since the images are very rare and fine
The mind cannot with clarity descry them all,
Except the one it strains to see.
The others pass away
All but the one the mind's prepared to see.
The mind prepares itself and hopes to see
The several images in natural consequence.
And just because the mind prepares itself,
The images arrive in this same consequence.
This too you must have seen:
When eyes begin to see things that are fine
They strain themselves, prepare.
Nor without this can eyes perceive the finer things with clarity.

And even when the object of our vision's plain to see,
You must have noticed this:—
Unless you turn your mind to them,
It's just as though the thing were far away,
And all the time were never there.
Why wonder then if mind misses all else,
Except those things which eager attentiveness
Compels the mind to see.
Then too, the human race
Often will base a broad belief on tiny bits of evidence
And so we wrap ourselves in snares of self-deceit.
It happens, too, from time to time
That images of different kind arise before the eyes;
What was a woman seems to become a man.
Familiar faces change to alien, unfamiliar forms
The young grows old; the old grows young.
Sleep and forgetfulness ensure
That none should hold this strange.

Avoid, I beg you, teleology

WITH all my heart I long that you should shun this fault of reasoning.
Through prudent fear and foresight in advance
This blunder miss:—
Don't ever think that eyes were made
In order that the human race might have the power to see.
Don't ever think that thighs or legs, based on the feet
Were made to bend that man might take long steps.
Don't ever think that forearms, joined to upper hands and arms
Were given us as servants either side
That we might do the things that serve our life.
Ideas like these which men proclaim are false in reasoning,
Abysmally confound effect with cause.
Nothing at all was brought to be in all our human frame

In order that the human race might use it;
What is brought to be creates its use.
Vision existed not at all
Before the light of eyes was brought to be;
Nor did men learn to pray in words before the tongue was brought
to be.

The tongue arrived much before speech;
Ears before sound was heard;
And all the human limbs I think
Were there before their use.
And so I think they have not come to be because of use.
That hands should clash in bloody battle strife
To mangle limbs and make the body foul with blood
All this was known before the shining darts
Shot through the air.
Nature made men avoid a wound, a blow,
Before the left arm, trained by art,
Held up a shield.
To lay the weary body down to rest
Is older far than soft-strewn beds;
To slake the thirst was known, long before cups.
And all these new discoveries found to suit the needs of life
Were found, one well believes, for sake of use.
The faculties were born quite differently;
First they evolved themselves and then revealed their use.
Among the latter we observe particularly the senses and the limbs.
And so, again, again, I say you can't, must not believe
That they were made for function of performing useful tasks.
Nor is this wonderful—that every living body seeks for food.
For I have shown
That many atoms stream and pass away from every thing,
But most must flow from living things.
For living things are worn to weariness

By ceaseless, pulsing motion every side.
And as they sweat, the atoms multitudinous
Are squeezed from deep within and carried out,
When living bodies pant in weariness.
By all these means the body waxes porous more and more,
Its strength is undermined.
Then pain is the result.
And so the creature takes in food to bolster up its limbs,
Renew its strength,
To fill the aching void, still the desire to eat,
Through all the veins and limbs.
And moisture spreads through all the spots where moisture is de-
sired.

And so the gathered forms of heat
Which set the guts on fire
Are blotted out by moisture streaming in,
Quenched like a flame.
The dry and parching heat cannot consume our limbs.
And so the panting and the thirst is washed away,
The craving passionate wish for food is satisfied.

How we can plant our feet and walk

How we can plant our feet and take a step,
When this is what we wish,
And how the gift is given men to move their limbs in various ways,
And what compulsion moves the body's mighty bulk,
This I must tell. You hearken to my words.
I say that first the image strikes upon the mind,
The impulse to proceed.
The image strikes upon the mind as I've just said.
And so the purpose comes—the will.
No man can do a thing, not anything,
Before the mind conceives what it will do,

Imagines in advance.
And what the mind foresees it does through images.
And so when mind bestirs itself,
Wishes to start and take a step,
It straightway strikes the power of soul,
The power that's scattered forth through all the limbs and frame.
This is an easy task since mind and soul are held in unity.
And then the soul goes forth and strikes the body utterly,
And bit by bit the whole vast bulk is pushed ahead and moves.
At times like this the body too is rarified,
And through the opened spaces rushes air,
(As rush it must since air is always quick to move)
And air abundant pushes through the passages,
Is scattered through the furthest, tiniest portions of the frame.
And so through these two causes acting separately,
It comes about that body moves,
As sailing ships are borne along by sails and wind.
Nor is this over-wonderful,
That forms so small can twist a frame so great,
And cause the mighty mass of matter in the frame to turn.
For thin-wrought wind of subtlest body made
Can push and drive a ship of mighty bulk,
And yet a single hand controls the ship,
No matter what the speed with which it moves,
The single hand can twist the single helm where'er it will.
A crane with pulleys and with drums
Can move a multitude of heavy things—
Haul them aloft with easy strain.

How sleep pours rest upon our limbs
and frees the mind from care

How sleep pours rest upon our limbs
And frees the mind from care,

This I proclaim in verses few, though sweet.
Just as the thin brief song of swans is sweeter far
Than clamor of the cranes—
The clamor spread abroad through southern clouds high in the sky.
Do you provide keen ear and eager mind,
Deny not what I say can be,
Or with a heart that shrinks from truth
Part company and lose yourself in error's swamp,
Or fail to see the path.
Sleep sinks on creatures when their strength of soul
Is scattered through the limbs,
And part of it has gone abroad, pushed on its way,
And part is pushed and driven deep within the frame.
And then, indeed, the limbs are loosened, droop.
Undoubtedly it's due to soul that consciousness resides in us,
When sleep takes consciousness from soul,
Then we must think that soul is all disturbed and cast outdoors.
And yet not all of soul.
For were this so the body would be bathed in death's eternal chill.
For if no part of soul lay hidden in the limbs,
As fire lurks choked and hidden under piles of ash,
How could the sudden flash of consciousness throughout the limbs
Blaze of a sudden, as flame can rise from hidden fire?
But how this change can come to pass,
And whence the soul can be disturbed and body slack,
This I'll explain. You let me not pour idle words upon the winds.
And first it has to be
That body on its outer side
Is pummelled well and buffeted by oft repeated blows,
Touched as it is—and close at hand—by breezes of the air.
Now almost every living thing on this account
Is covered in—
By hide or shells, callous or bark.

Moreover as the creatures breathe
Their inner side is equally assailed by this same air,
Alternately drawn in, breathed out again.
Now since the body is on both sides buffeted—inside and out—
And since the blows can penetrate the pores,
And touch the inner, tiny atom stuff,
There soon occurs
A gradual, imperceptible decaying of the limbs.
The atom structure of the mind is shaken and confused.
The inner portion of the soul is hurled abroad;
The outer part retreats and hides within.
And part throughout the limbs is torn,
Cannot unite or interact in movements mutual.
For nature bars its meetings, blocks its ways.
And therefore consciousness departs
Through changes of its motion, deep within.
And since there's nothing now, can serve them as a prop—
Support the limbs—
Weak grows the body, all the limbs grow faint,
The arms and eyelids droop;
Thighs, at the very time you lay you down to sleep
Often collapse, and all their power dissolves.
Again, sleep often follows food.
For food's effect, when spread throughout the veins,
Is just the same as air's;
The sleep you take when stuffed with food,
Or when you're very tired
Is deepest sleep.
More atom forms disturb themselves, bruised by great toil.
For this cause too,
The soul at times like these
Is pushed deep down within the frame,
Is strown abroad more lavishly,

Is torn asunder, broken up the more,
Within the frame.

On dreams

Now generally the tasks that men pursue in waking life,
The tasks to which the spirit clings and cleaves,
To which the mind devotes its time,
And raises every power of life to highest, tensest stretch,
To these same tasks a man in sleep
Will also give himself.
A lawyer pleads his case in dreams,
Draws up the draft of laws.
The soldiers enter battle's shock and fight;
And sailors wage a lonely battle with the winds;
Just as I seem in dreams to wrestle with philosophy,
Search Nature's laws and set them forth—
To live for evermore, in verses formed in native Latin tongue.
So every art and every interest
Holds captive minds deluded during sleep.
And if for many days a man has turned his eager mind
To gladiatorial combats or the stage,
We often see that though the show has ceased,
The pores and passages of mind are open none the less,
Through which the images of games may enter in.
And so for many days the self same spectacles
Will dance before their eyes.
Nay even with their waking eyes imagination makes them see
The actors in the dance, moving their supple limbs.
Even with waking ears,
They hear the liquid chant of lyre, its sonorous strings.
They see the actors grouped to play their parts,
And all the varied splendour of the stage;
So strong the power of pleasure and delight,

So powerful is the sway of interest—
The tasks to which mankind devotes its strength.
Not men alone!
The same holds true for every living animal.
Often you'll see a mighty horse, though limbs are lulled in sleep,
Sweat in its dreams and pant
And strain with every fibre, might and main,
To win the victory.
The hounds of hunters, too, though locked in gentle sleep,
Still throw their legs about, still suddenly give tongue,
Still sniff the breezes time and time again,
As though they'd found and followed hard the scent of prey,
As though awake to follow empty images of deer,
See them in eager flight.
Until the vision fades, error departs;
They gain their true and waking selves once more.
And fawning puppies reared at home,
Are swift to shake their bodies, raise them from the ground,
As if they saw an unfamiliar form or face.
Much more the wilder things.
The wilder is the breed,
The more it rages, tosses, tumbles in its dreams.
And various tribes of birds fly off,
With sudden rising in the still of night,
Disturb the sacred groves of gods
With whirr of wings;
If in their gentle sleep they dream of hawk's fell swoop
The fight and murderous battle that hawks bring.
Then too, the human mind which moving mightily performs great
                                                        things
Often in sleep may do and dare the same.
Kings they will capture, themselves be captive led,
Create a mimic show of war in dreams

Cry out that murder's imminent,
Yet never leave their place.
And men will struggle hard and groan in pain,
And fill the place with anguished shrieks,
As if the teeth of panthers met in tender flesh,
Or savage lion.
And many in their sleep discourse of high affairs,
Or testify to their own guilt;
Many meet death.
Many are gripped with panic fear,
Dreaming they fall from lofty towers or mountain tops.
And these as though with mind distraught sometimes find it hard
To come again to waking and to consciousness;
They wake all trembling both in heart and limb.
And many a man who dreams of thirst
Will sit beside a stream or pleasant spring
And gulp in wild imagining the flooding river down his thirsty
throat.

And often people who in waking life are clean,
As though unbuttoning at a toilet or a wayside urinal,
Will pour the bladder's filtered liquid forth,
And soak the lovely, costly coverlets from Babylon.

The boy's young dream of love

AND boys who're passing into puberty
When ripening time has filled their vessels with the reproductive
seed,

May see in sleep the lovely images of female forms—
A glorious face, a lovely colouring,
Which stir their vessels laden with love's seed,
And makes them pour it forth as if in consummation of desire,
To wet the blankets and defile their clothes.

On love

THIS of which we spoke before,
Is stirred in boys when manhood's coming strengthens human
limbs.
For different things by different causes are provoked and roused.
In man its only human charm can stir the vital seed,
And when it leaves its place, issues from its abode,
From every human part it comes and finds its rendezvous,
Stirs up the genitals.
These are aroused and swollen with the seed
Until the impulse comes to drive it forth,
To plant it in the lovely form;
Body seeks body as the mind is stirred with love.
A wounded man will generally fall towards the wound.
The blood spurts out to meet the blow.
(If he is near at hand the red stream stains the foe.)
Just so in love.
A man is wounded with the love Queen's dart—
By boy with girlish limbs,
By woman breathing passion from her whole expanse.
Just like the wounded man he falls towards the thing that caused
the wound.
He tries to join himself to that—to leave the vital flood in that belovéd
form.
For voiceless passion is an augury of pleasure that's to come.

This pleasure, then, is love for us, thence comes the name

THIS pleasure, then, is love for us, thence comes the name.
Hence, first of all,
The drops of Love's sweet passion into heart distilled
Are followed by cold care.
Though she, beloved object, is afar,

179

Yet pictures of her haunt the eyes;
Her lovely name, the ears.
And yet it's best to banish love's imaginings
And fast from food of love; turn the mind elsewhere,
Indulge your lust with anyone at hand,
Not focus it on one and so pile up
Mountains of grief assured.
The sore will grow and fester if you feed it.
Day by day the madness grows, the pang more piercing,
Unless love's wounds you scramble with fresh strokes,
And loiter after ladies of the streets,
Before you're chained to one
(Unless in studies new you can absorb the mind).
He who shuns love does not lose love's reward.
He picks a pleasure less alloyed with pain.
For surely pleasure's purer when you're fancy free.
And lover's passion even at possession's hour,
Tosses about in dark, blind blundering.
He hesitates what first he should enjoy with hand or eye.
What they have pursued they tightly squeeze,
And cause the body pain,
And often fasten teeth in lips, smite mouth with kisses—
The pleasure is not pure and secret goads lurk there,
Bidding them hurt whate'er it be that has induced their madness.
But Venus gently mitigates these pains in love:
Sweet pleasure mingled checks the bites.
Here is his hope that passion can be quenched,
Even by the body that induced the flame.
But nature objects and makes it happen just the other way.
Alone of human appetites love is like this:
The more it feeds, the fiercer flames desire.
For food and drink are taken in the limbs,
Possessing their allotted part of human frame;

Desire for them is easily assuaged.
But from the lovely face, complexion fair of loved one
Nothing the lover gleans for pleasure save some pictured images,
At which fond hope doth grasp like straws in wind.
Just as in dreams a thirsty man may long to drink,
But water is not there to quench his thirst,
He strives in vain to grasp at water's images,
And still feels pangs of thirst,
The while he thinks he drinks from torrent stream
Just so in love, Venus mocks lovers with these images;
They cannot sate their lust through gazing on love's form.
And though his hands move aimless over all,
He cannot wring a piece from lovely limbs.
Even when at the last,
Lovers embrace and taste the flower of youth,
Sweet augury of coming bliss
When Venus plants her seed in female form,
With eagerness they press, body to body, lip to lip,
And intermingle moisture from their mouths,
'Tis all in vain.
He cannot shave away a fragment from beloved flesh
Or bury life in passion of a mutual ecstasy.
Just this at times they seem to wish to do,
So gladly are they held in Venus's bonds,
While limbs grow loose and liquid in love's ecstasy.
And when accumulated lust has left their limbs,
A little while they feel a respite from desire.
They cannot find device to conquer their disease;
In doubt they waste away from secret wounds.
Think too,
They dissipate their strength and spend their energy.
They pass their life under another's sway.
Work is neglected, name and fame grow sick and faint.

Fortune meanwhile is spent, lavished on eastern scents,
Corinthian shoes, dainty and sweet, to grace a lady's feet.
Yes, and great emeralds flashing green are set in gold.
The lover's ardor constantly wears out
The sheer and purple gown.
(It's used too hard and drinks up Venus' sweat).
Their wealth is spent in bands and ribbons for the hair
Islands and mainlands send out their gorgeous stuffs.
Wealth is poured out on linens, dainties for the feast,
Games, frequent toasts, perfumes, garlands and wreaths.
But all in vain, for from the fount of charms,
There ever flows a bitter drop even 'mid the flowers,—
Some pang of conscience, surging of remorse,
That life should pass in idling and in wantonness.
The lady, perhaps, has dropped a headless word
To torture him and left its sense in doubt—
A word that lodged in lover's consciousness
And burned to flame.
Or else he finds her eyes too restless fears another man;
Or finds a gleam of malice in her smile.
Even when love goes well these problems rise.
But when love's crossed and hopeless, torments countless throng,
Which you could see in darkness with shut eyes.
So it is better far exactly as I've cautioned you,
To be on guard beforehand, be on guard, be not enticed.
To shun entanglement in snares of love,
That's not so difficult.
But once entangled in its mesh, to break away again,
And burst the bonds of love's entanglement—
That's hard.
But even when you're caught within the snare of love
You still might get away, escape,
Unless you block yourself

By missing all the blemishes of body and of mind
In her you seek and woo.
For men are generally by passion swayed,
Assigning every virtue to a girl,
Which is not truly hers.
And so we often see an ugly girl, a girl deformed,
The object of man's love, blindly admired.
And sometimes friend may laugh at friend,
Bid him appease the savage god of love,
And realize that his friend is smitten with a passion very base,
But his own greater ills, poor fool, he fails to see.
And so a dark-complexioned girl may be described
As 'Honey-dark.'
A girl who's foul and filthy in her ways,
As unadorned;
A green-eyed girl—'Athena's other self.'
A wooden, skinny girl is called 'gazelle.'
A plump and stubby girl 'Incarnate grace,'
And 'all pure wit.'
A large ungainly one 'a marvel and a walking majesty.'
If ceaseless stammering impede her speech
'She has a lisp.'
If silent through stupidity her 'modest bearing' is admired.
A nagging spiteful gossip 'Virtue's very torch.'
Another wasting right away and on the point of death,
Is called 'a slender wisp of love.'
And if she's nearly dead with bronchial cough,
Her lover calls her 'frail.'
The lady with the ample breasts is known as 'Ceres' self.'
The girl with nose upturned,
'Silenus and a Satyr.'
The thick-lipped girl 'a living kiss.'
Other examples of the kind were tedious to tell.

But granted that she's truly fair,
That Venus breathes desire from every limb,
Are there not others just as fair?
Have we not lived before she came to view?
Does she not do as well or badly in the act of love
As any ugly girl?
Does she not reek of cheap perfume
To move her maids to giggles and to furtive mirth?
But, when the door slams in his face the lover weeps,
And piles the steps and entrance with a mound of flowers,
Adorns the haughty posts that line the door
With aromatic herbs.
And in his folly even plants unending kisses on the doors.
But if the girl should yield to his insistent importunity,
One whiff would be enough.
He'd seek some honest cause to take his hasty leave;
The plaintive elegy he'd spent so long composing,
He'd toss away;
And curse himself and call himself a silly fool
Because she'd won from him
This deep devotion—more than any mortal woman should.
All this is known to all the female devotees of love.
That's why they want to draw a decent veil of reticence
Over the arts of love;
Nor let him see the tricks
Whom they want caught and fettered in the toils of love.
But all in vain since you—albeit only mentally—
Can draw all tricks to light,
Investigate the cause of all the merriment.
Besides, assuming that the lady's reasonable,
And not a spiteful mind,
You can forgive some faults in turn,
Be tolerant of human frailties.

Nor are a woman's sighs of passion always feigned;
With lovers' forms entwined, embracing limb to limb,
Often she gives her heart to it and yearns for mutual love.
She woos the male that both should run alike the course of mutual
ecstasy.

Birds, cattle, beasts, both wild and tame,
Could not endure the onslaught of the male
Unless their nature also were afire,
Were full to overflowing with the welling flame of love,
And gladly meets the ardent passion of the male.
Do you not often see how those who're bound in ties of mutual love
Are cruelly tortured by the common bond?
Sometimes where two roads cross
Two dogs are locked together in the sturdy bonds of love.
They long to part and go their several ways,
They tug and strain, but fruitlessly,
And this would never be unless they knew the joy of mutual ecstasy,
To coax them into pain and hold them fast in passion's bonds.
And so insist I must
Love's pleasure is a mutual thing.
And often in the act of intercourse,
When woman's sudden power has gripped the power of the male,
Then through the strength of female seeds,
Children resemble her;
Just as through the strength of father's seed,
Children resemble him.
And sometimes you will see
Children who draw their forms and features from the two.
And these, of course, are sprung from father's body and from
mother's blood;
When mutual passion in a mutual breath,
Has dashed together seeds aroused throughout the limbs,
By stimulus of love;

And neither was by partner's passion overcome.
Sometimes, too the new-begotten child
Resembles an ancestor—
Grandparents, or even others even more remote;
The atom forms, you see, are variously concealed and mingled in
the parent stock.
And these are passed from far remote antiquity
From father onto father onto son.
And from this atom stuff,
In great kaleidoscopic lottery
The goddess, presiding queen of love,
Unfolds the various forms,
Recalls the looks, the voice, the hair
Of ancestors remote;
Since these no less than faces, bodies, limbs
Are made from growth of predetermined seeds.
The female sex can spring from father's seed,
From mother's body too, can come the male.
All creatures from the union of two seeds are formed,
Their looks recall the dominant.
This you can see yourself,
Whether you test a male or female child.
Nor is it gods who give to man a barren seed,
Ensure that no sweet children call him 'Dad,'
Compelling such a man to, pass his life in wedlock's sterile bonds.
Even though many men believe just this,
And in their sorrow sprinkle altars of the gods with streams of
blood and fire,
And pile up gifts in lofty temples of the holy ones,
To make their wives conceive.
In vain they weary godhead and its awful fates.
For procreation is denied to many for a natural cause.
In some the seed's too thick;

In some too liquid, overthin.
The thin seed cannot find its proper anchorage,
Trickles away too soon, and fails to cause conception of a child.
The thick seed sometimes fails to dash towards its goal,
Or cannot penetrate as well the vital spots,
Or mingles badly with the female seed.
Loves unions are very various.
Some men make certain women easily conceive;
Some women take their load of pregnancy more easily from certain
men.

A woman who in earlier unions always failed,
May find a mate with whom she easily conceives,
And comes to know the rich affection of a child.
And many men have married wives of proved fertility,
Yet failed with them;
Until they find the proper union and beget their kind,
Create a sturdy fortress for advancing age.
So vital it is that the seeds should mix,
In procreative fashion—the thick with liquid,
Liquid with thick.
The diet is important, too.
On some foods seeds will swell within the limbs,
On other foods grow thin and weak.
And how the pleasant sexual act is carried out,
This is important, too.
It's generally held that women best conceive,
When intercourse takes place in fashion of a quadruped;
The seed best penetrates when breasts are low and buttocks up.
Wives do not need in intercourse
Voluptuous movements, wanton ecstasy.
With these a woman tends to block conception,
If in spite of passion's ecstasy
She draws her buttocks back from passion of the male,

Receives the moisture with her frame relaxed,
She drives the furrow of the share
Far from its proper way.
The onslaught of the semen does not reach the place it should.
These motions harlots make and think them in their interest,
That so they fail to take the seed, escape a pregnancy,
And also that the act of intercourse be pleasanter for men;
But neither end is needed by our wives.
It's not divine decree or supernatural ordering,
That helps an ugly woman win man's love.
A girl can often win her prize herself
By modest bearing and by neat array.
Easy you'll come to think you'd find
A life with girl like this.
Is not a stern resolve by frequent little blows worn down?
The hardest rock in time's long span will crack and wear away
If frequent blows of water keep on pounding it.

Book Five

In praise of Epicurus who first brought philosophy to
bear on the ordering of human life

WHAT TALENT'S ADEQUATE, and what poetic powers,
   To match the insight of this seer's philosophy?
Or whose command of words is great enough to match his worth,
Deserve the gifts he's given from heart and brain?
No mortal, as I think.
If I can speak as demonstrated majesty of theme demands,
He was a god, a god, I say, O Memmius renowned.
He first brought reason's gifts to man's life's ordering
(That which we've come to call philosophy.)
His thought has brought the barque of human life
Out of the billows, lodged it safe in port;
Out of the inky black and stress of midnight storm
Placed it in clear and calm and dazzling light.
Could any god accomplish more than this?
Think of the other gifts we call divine.
Ceres, the legend states, brought grain to men, and Bacchus, wine.
Without these gifts man's life can still go on.
Distant tribes, they say, have never needed them.
Without a mind at peace no man lives well.
And so 'tis right that we should think him god,
Whose consolations known afar, bring peace of mind.

If you think Hercules a greater benefactor of mankind,
You're clearly wrong.
What damage could Nemaean lion with yawning jaws
Or bristling boar of Arcady do to mankind?
Or Cretan bull, or hydra with its palisade of poisonous snakes,
Or three fold might of triple bodied Geryon?
Or those foul birds that have their home
In the Stymphalian marsh?
Or those wild steeds of Diomede the Thracian,
Horses whose nose breathes flame
Beside the streams of Bistones and Ismara?
Or that fierce dragon with the fiery looks,
Who guards the golden apples of th' Hesperides?
That monstrous beast whose loathsome form
Twines round the stout tree trunk,
What harm could he have done mankind
Besides the Ocean's grim expanse,
Besides Atlantic's far resounding shore,
Where none of us now dares to go,
And no barbarian ever dares?
And all the other monsters of this kind which were destroyed;
But even were they not,
What harm, I say could they have done alive?
No harm, at all.
Even to day earth teems with terror and with savage beasts,
In glades and mighty mountains and deep woods.
Their haunts we can avoid, if that's our wish.
But if the heart's not pure, what perils and what wars
We have to enter, if we wish or not!
What pangs of care can rive an anxious heart!
What terrors, too!
And what of pride and lust and wantonness!
And what of luxury and sloth!

And so the seer who banished all these sins
By words, not arms,
Should we not number him among th' immortal gods?
And this the more because he used to speak in good and godlike
words
About the gods themselves,
And by his reasoning reveal the stuff of things.

My task in this book

I FOLLOW in his footsteps, think his thoughts,
And teach by what stern law all things are made,
And how they must abide in it,
Nor break the strong decrees of time.
First of all the mind, we've learned consists of mortal stuff,
Unable to endure through endless time,
Though visions do in sleep perplex and cheat the mind:
(We seem to see the dead who've lived their life.)

The universe once came to be and sometime it will die

Now the unfolding of my thought brings this point next:
I must show the cosmos likewise made of mortal stuff,
And how the meeting of material particles,
Created earth and sky and sea and stars and moon and sun.
And then what living creatures came to be on earth,
And what could never be.
And how men learned to speak,
Communicating thought in various tongues
By naming things.
How fear of gods has entered human hearts,
A fear which round the world keeps places holy,
Fanes and lakes and groves, altars and images of gods.
And then I will expound
The wanderings of the sun, the paths of moon,

How steersman Nature governs them.
So we'll not think spontaneously or free of will
They move on yearly courses, well-disposed to man,
Producing crops and creatures for his need.
And most of all not think that blessed Providence
Could move the years and seasons.
For even men who've fully learned that gods lead care-free lives,
If ignorant of laws by which things move,
Those things in chief which happen overhead, up in the sky,
They're drawn to ancient creed and cult again;
Imagine savage tyrants overhead
Strong to accomplish anything;
Because, poor fools,
They know not what can come to be and what cannot,
The law that binds each thing, its deep-set boundary stone.

The sea, the lands, the sky one day will hurtle down to ruin

Now for the rest, no longer dallying with promises,
Consider first: the seas, the land, the sky,
Three natures, triple-body, triple-form so much alike
One day, my friend, in just one day will hurtle down to ruin.
The massive structure of the universe
That lasted many years will fall apart.
I know full well how strange a thing,
Stupendous to the mind is this my doctrine,
That earth and sky will one day fall in ruin.
How hard it is for words like these of mine
To win belief!
It's always so when novel thought assails the mind;
Ideas beyond the reach of sight and touch
Which always give the easiest access to the heart and temples of the
mind.
But speak I will.

Maybe the very fact will bring belief—
Perhaps you'll feel an earthquake, see the earth,
The whole earth shaken in a moment's time.
May pilot Fortune steer us from this fate;
May thought, not horror, make us realize
The whole might fall one day in rending, sounding crash.
Before I approach this point, tell destiny, more certainly,
More sacredly, than Pythian priestess
Speaking from the laurelled shrine
And tripod of the Delphic god,
I've many consolations to unfold in verse.
So will you not,
Checked by the bridle bit of ancient creed,
Think earth and sky and sun, and sea and stars and moon,
Because divine in structure, must endure
Through endless time.
So you'll not think it right
That man, like giants rebellious, should torments face,
For shaking with his thought the walls of universe
Wanting to quench the glorious sun in Heaven,
Branding immortal fact with mortal speech.
These things are not divine,
Not worthy to be numbered with the gods;
Rather they give us hint of what is far removed
From living motion and from consciousness.

Soul and mind cannot be without a body to encompass them

WE surely cannot think that mind and consciousness
Are linked with every thing material;
Trees cannot live in air, nor clouds in salty sea,
Nor fish in fields, nor blood in logs, nor sap in stones.
Fixed law ordains where each thing lives and grows.

So mind can never be without the brain,
No consciousness apart from blood and cells.
For if it could it's far more plausible
That mind should lurk in head or shoulders,
Even in the heels or any other part of man;
At least the human vase remains the same.

The world was not created by gods

THIS, too, it cannot be that you believe
That holy places of the gods exist
In some remote abode of this great universe.
The nature of the gods is very fine
And from the grasp of human sense
Far, far, removed;
Nay scarcely to be grasped by power of human mind.
Now since the godhead is thus far below
The touch or blow of human hands,
It cannot touch whatever we find touchable.
(Nothing can touch which cannot in its turn be touched.)
Thus the abodes and seats of mighty gods
Cannot resemble ours.
They're rather rare and fine as gods themselves are fine.
All this I'll later prove with bounteous floods of argument.
And then to say that for the sake of man
The will of god brought forth the glorious universe,
And therefore man should praise this glorious work of god,
All worthy of all praise;
Hold that creation always was and always will endure;
To think it impious ever to shake in its eternal haunts
Assail with human arguments or overwhelm it utterly
What once for endless time
Was by the ancient wisdom of the deity

Established for the human race;
To think all this, pile up a mountainous argument,
Is foolishness, my friend.
What profit could our gratitude ensure to blessed and immortal gods,
That they attempt a favour for the sake of man?
Or after all the previous ages of tranquillity
What novelty could prompt a god to change his mode of life.
For only those can long for fundamental change,
To whom the old was not endurable.
For these immortal ones
Who never felt the pang of pain throughout the past,
Who lived a lovely life,
How could desire for basic change enkindle these?
What was so bad for mortal man if he were never born?
Or did our life lie foully prone, in darkness and in grief,
Until creation's primal day had dawned on it?
But once a man is born,
He needs must wish to stay alive
So long as joy of life has hold of him.
But he who never was alive
Who never tasted for himself the love of life,
How does it harm someone like this
That he was never made?
How was the pattern for creating things implanted in the gods?
How came the notion of humanity,
That gods should know and mentally conceive
That which they would create?
How could the power of atom stuff ever be known?
And all the rich variety of things that atom force can bring to be
By fresh arrangement of the particles,
If Mother Nature had not given
A demonstration of creative power?

Rather the clashing of the atoms brought the universe to be

RATHER in numbers infinite atoms move in many ways,
Throughout the whole immense expanse of space,
They're beaten and they're buffeted,
From infinite time in blind experiment essay
All movements and all meetings,
And so it is not wonderful that they should come
To this exact arrangement of atomic shapes
To these same movements out of which the present sum of things is
made.

The imperfections in the world prove that it was not created by divine providence

BUT even if I knew nothing of the atom stuff,
This I would dare affirm—
By thinking on the very laws of sky,
And prove with wealth of argument—
The universe has not been made by power divine,
It holds too many flaws.
Of all the earth that's covered by the vast expanse of sky,
A greedy half is held by mountains and the forest homes of beasts,
Rocks and vast swamps,
The sea that holds apart the shores of continents.
Almost two thirds is kept from human use
By burning desert heat or endless frost.
And what remains
Nature's resistless force would choke with weeds,
If constant human toil did not resist,—
Men who gain their livelihood
By pressing firmly on the plough,
By constant labour with the restless hoe;
Unless we turn the fertile sod with iron plough,

Subdue the soil,
The crops would not spring up to liquid air,
Spontaneously.
And even when by constant toil we've raised a crop,
The fields are green and all a-flower,
The sun in sky will parch with too much heat,
Or sudden rains wreck havoc, or chill frosts,
Or blasts of violent winds in headlong hurricane,
And why should nature rear and nurture savage beasts
To harm the race of man on land and sea?
Why do the changing seasons of the year bring pestilence?
And why does early death stalk everywhere?
The infant boy lies naked on the ground,
Like sailor cast ashore by savage seas,
And lacks all aid for life,
When Nature first has cast him forth
By travail from his mother's womb,
And all the place around he fills with piteous wail,
As is most natural
Since endless troubles face the child in life.
But various beasts both wild and tame
Grow to maturity,
And have no need of childish toys—
The rattle or the rocking horse,
Or kindly nurse's broken baby talk.
Nor do they need to change their clothes
To suit the season of the year;
Nor armaments nor lofty walls to guard their young.
The earth herself brings forth all needful things,
Abundantly;
The earth and Nature—creative queen of everything.
Now since the body of the earth and sea
The soft caressing breezes, summer's heat

That go to make the sum of things,
All these are made of body that knows birth and death,
It follows that the universe consists of mortal stuff.
For if the limbs and parts of anything
Are made of mortal stuff,
It follows that the whole must too.
And when accordingly,
We see the mighty members and constituent parts of all the universe
Consumed away and brought to birth again,
We know that sky and earth
Began one day, one day will end.

The various parts of the universe are subject to change and decay.
a) The Earth

Now lest you think that in this argument,
I arbitrarily snatch at proof,
Assume that earth and fire are mortal things,
And do not doubt that air and moisture die,
Are born again in turn and grow,
Consider this:
Some portion of the surface of the earth
When parched by ceaseless sun,
Or trampled by the tread of countless feet,
Gives off a murk and flying clouds of dust,
Which blasts of stormy winds bear through the air.
Some portion of its sod is summoned back to swamp by rains,
Eroding streams tear at the river bank,
And whatsoever earth nurtures and rears
To earth returns in turn.
And since assuredly,
The universal mother is the universal tomb of things
So you may know

That earth herself is worn away in turn,
In turn increases, grows.

b) *Water*

Now for the rest,
We need not words to prove
That oceans, rivers, streams
With moisture new are ever filled,
That endless waters always trickle down,
The mighty torrent waterfalls on every side
Are proof enough.
The water near at hand is pulled away—
There's never excess moisture in the total universe.
The strong fresh squalls that sweep the sea
Diminish it,
The sun above unravels it,
But none of it is lost in passing through the earth,
Brine is filtered off, the moisture trickles back,
Assembles at the source of every stream,
Thence flows through earth in torrent fresh
Wherever once a way is cut
To let the waters run in liquid march.

c) *Air*

AND then I speak of air
Which changes in a thousand different ways,
Each single hour.
For all that flows from any thing
Is carried to the mighty sea of air.
Unless this sea of air in turn
Gave substance back to things,
Renewed their flow, assuredly,

The universe by now would be resolved
And turned to air.
And so it never fails to be
That air is turned to things, and things to air,
And all things never cease to flow.

d) Fire and the sun

Likewise the bounteous fount of liquid light,
The sun above,
Fails not to flood the sky with brightness new,
As new light straightway takes the place of light.
The light that's in the forefront ever dies,
Where'er it strikes.
A proof is this:
When first a cloud has passed beneath the sun
Broken its rays,
The lower broken part of these same rays,
Must straightway die and all the earth,
Wherever clouds obstruct the sun
Is dark.
From this you learn
That radiance must always be renewed;
That light that's in the forefront ever dies.
Unless the radiance were renewed.
Nothing in daylight could be seen,
Unless the very source of light gave light unendingly.
Then too, the lights of earth,
The hanging lamp, the oily torch,
Bright with its shimmering light
And dark with murky smoke,
Just like the sun provide new light;
In eagerness to flicker with their flames,
In eagerness, I say.

Nor ever does the almost-interrupted light desert the place,
So quickly is its death supplied from all the fires,
By swift new birth of flame.
And therefore we must think
That sun and moon and stars
Keep hurling light from ever fresh supply of light;
The light that's in the forefront ever dies.
And so you'll never think them strong with strength invincible.

   Buildings, too, decay

AGAIN you see
That stones are vanquished by the power of time,
That lofty towers fall in ruins, rocks decay,
That holy images of gods and sacred shrines
Grow weary, worn and faint with time;
Nor can the holy power of god extend the bounds of fate,
Contend against creative nature and her laws.
Then too, we see the monuments of mighty men decay,
And in the process of decay mutely enquire,
Whether you think they're growing old.
And boulders, too, torn from lofty hills roll down,
Unable to endure the power and strength of even finite time;
Nor suddenly,
Would they be torn away and fall
If they could bear without a break
Time's endless torments from infinity.
Consider now the sky,
Which in its large embrace, above, around,
Grasps all our earth.
If, as some think,
This sky begets all nature from itself
And takes again into itself
All things at death;

Then all of sky itself must know
Both birth and death.
Whatever from itself can rear and nurture other things,
Must suffer increase, lessening in turn.
Then too, if earth and sky did not begin in time,
Why have not other poets sung of glorious deeds,
Before the Theban wars, before the fall of Troy?
Why have so many other deeds of men
So often passed away,
And never left a monument of endless fame?
As I believe,
Our universe is new, the sum of things is young,
But recently began.
And therefore other arts even to this day,
Still grow, are polished to perfection's peak;
The art of seamanship is growing up.
But recently the men of music have brought forth
New and resounding harmonies.
Then too this art of mine—this study of philosophy,
Discovery of Nature's laws, is new.
I was the first to put it into Latin speech.
Now if you think that all these arts were known before;
But human life was blotted out in some spectacular, mighty con-
                                                    flagration,
And civil arts destroyed in some upheaval of the world;
Or rivers, swollen by perpetual rains,
Have ravaged countryside alike and towns,
Then even more you must admit and own,
That earth and sky as well will one day have an end.
For when we find a thing oppressed by mighty maladies,
And perils sore,
We ought to know,
That if a cause more sinister assailed,

Great and far reaching were the crash
Of this same thing.
This is the proof that we are born to die
That one by one we fall a prey to those same maladies,
Which once assailed the dead.
Another thought:

What alone could be immortal

IF anything could remain for evermore,
It must be through its strong solidity,
A strength to beat back every blow,
Repel and keep away all influence and force,
That might unlock the close-bound parts within.
The atom forms which I discussed before will illustrate this truth.
Or else it can endure through endless time,
Because it knows no blows—
I'll cite as illustration, void,
Which evermore abides unharmed, untouched,
And cannot suffer anything from any outer force;
Or else because there is no space around,
In which the thing might part asunder or be broken up;
Or else because there is nothing material outside,
To hit and smash them with a mighty blow.
But as I've proved long since,
The nature of the universe is not of solid form,
Since in its parts there's always space in-mixed.
Nor is it like the void.
Bodies are lurking there which might one day by chance
Collect together from infinity
And overwhelm our total universe
In one grand blinding crash,
Or smash it utterly some other way.
And space is there, extending to infinity

In which the ramparts of the universe
Might perish, smashed by any other force.
The awful gate of death is then not shut,
In sky, on sun or earth, or in the ocean deeps.
It yawns and looks on mortal things
With quite portentous maw.
And so confess you must
That all the total universe has had a birth;
For nothing made of mortal stuff could from infinity
Be strong, endure the sturdy power of endless time.
Then too, the various, mighty fragments of the universe
With one another fight so furiously,
In most unholy war aroused,
Do you not see that some end must be set,
To this long war?
It may be when the sun and heat of every kind
Have drunk up all the moisture in the universe and won the day.
Now this they try to do, so far without success;
So great the store of water that the rivers give.
And rivers in their turn are always threatening
To exceed their bounds, overwhelm the universe
With water from the Ocean's depths.
But all in vain;
The winds that sweep the watery wastes, dry up the ocean,
And the rays of sun break moisture down, unravel it.
And these two powers allied
Feel confident that they can make things dry
Before the force of water could come near
The ending of its task.
For these two elements
Breathe mighty war in even-poiséd fight,
And strive together for a mastery of mighty things.
Yet once of old in this continuing fight

Fire gained the upper hand.
And once, so legend goes,
The waters reigned in all the fields.

The legend of Phaethon

FIRE won its way and burned up many things—
Fire all-devouring with its licking flames,
When th' headlong might of horses of the sun
Ranged far,
And carried Phaethon through the width of sky,
To traverse every land.
The almighty father then in piercing wrath aroused
With sudden thunderbolt,
Dashed Phaethon from his chariot to the earth.
And as he fell and met the sun,
Phaethon caught up the everburning torch of all the universe
And tamed the scattered trembling steeds,
And put the yoke on them, and guided them along their proper path,
And thus replenished all things.
At least this tale the ancient poets of Greece have sung.
It's far removed from logic and from truth.
For fire can only then prevail
When many bodies of the fire's material stuff
Have risen from unending space.
Either then the strength of fire must fail
In some way overcome;
Or else the objects of the fire are burned, scorched by its fiery blasts.
And once the waters rose, or so the legend goes,
Began to win, and vanquished countless towns of men.
But after that,
When water's power in some way turned aside, receded, went its
way,—

The sum of all the water gathered from all infinity—
The rain then ceased to fall, the rivers lost their might.

*The movement of matter, not design or fiat of foreseeing mind, has
made the universe*

COME now, I will expound in due array,
How meetings of material particles
Established sky and earth and ocean's deeps,
And courses of the sun and moon.
Assuredly,
Not by design or fiat of foreseeing mind
Did atoms set themselves in ordered ranks
Nor did they make a compact or arrange
Which movements each should start.
Rather the multitudinous atom shapes
From endless time in fashions infinite
Were driven on by mutual blows
Until this very day.
And carried downward by their weight were born along,
United every way, and tried in every way
That so they might create the universe of things,
By joining each to each.
And so it comes about
That scattered as they are through endless time,
Every kind of motion and of meeting they explore;
At last and suddenly those atom forms unite
And this their meeting which often forms the starting points
For mighty things—
For earth and sky and sea and every race of living things.
The sun that moves on high with bounteous light,
Before the joining of the atom forms
Could not be seen;
No, nor the constellations of the mighty universe,

No sea, nor sky, nor earth, nor air,
Nothing of all the things we know.
The universe was like a newly risen massive storm
Composed of every kind of atom particle.
The strife of these, confusion in the interspaces,
Confusion in their paths, their meetings, weights and blows,
Confusion in their movements and their contactings
The strife of these brought wars.
For owing to their different forms and various shapes,
They could not keep their unity as now they do,
And give and get between themselves
Their proper mutual motions.
Now from this primal mass
A portion would depart, this side and that,
And like began to join with like,
And so reveal a world;
And separate constituent parts,
And set its elements apart—
I mean, divide the deep of sky from lands; and both from sea.
That sea might flow around the solid world,
With moisture sundered from the solid land;
Likewise the fires of sky,
Set by themselves unmixed and kept apart.
At first you see
The various bodies of the earth,
Because tight interlaced with heavy weight,
United in the centre of the primal storm
And occupied the lowest place
And as they met and interlaced
The more they pressed out atom forms
To make the sea and stars and sun and moon,
And ramparts of the mighty universe.
For all of these are made of smoother, rounder atom seeds,

Of atom forms much smaller than is earth.
And so the fiery aether rose up first,
Bursting from the corners of the earth through scattered pores
And, as it rose, took off and bore along uncounted fires.
Just as we often see when first the golden morning light of radiant
sun

Sheds flames of red over the dew pearled grass,
While pools and running streams give off a mist,
And even earth herself at times is seen to steam;
When all these streams of mist converge above,
Then clouds with shapes now made weave patterns in the sky;
Even so in primal times the spreading aether all around was placed
With shapes now formed
And spread to every part of universe on every side,
And fenced all other things around in eager greedy grasp.

Origin of the sun and moon

From this arose the first beginnings of the sun and moon,
Those cosmic spheres which turn in air midway between,—
Spheres which almighty aether could not claim, nor earth could
claim,

Not heavy enough to sink and settle to the earth,
Nor light enough to glide along the topmost shores;
And yet are placed between
To move as living forms and take their place
As portions of the total universe.
Just as in our human frame some limbs stand while others move.
And so when elements that formed the aether, sun and moon
Were once withdrawn the earth sank suddenly;
Where now extends the mighty blue expanse of sea
To flood each ditch with salt sea surge.
And day by day the more that aethers' surging tides
And sun's hot rays

With constant blows on every side made earth close packed;
The blows around its whole circumference made earth contract
And at its centre grow more dense;
So much the more did salty sweat, squeezed from the earth,
Ooze out, increase the sea and swimming plains.
Likewise the more did atom forms of heat and air
Slip out and fly abroad;
Until, condensing far from earth
They made the lofty, gleaming temples of the sky.
And then the level plains sank down;
The slopes of mighty hills increased.
(The rocks, you see, could not sink down,
Nor could all parts of earth subside,
In equal fashion, equally.)

Origin of earth

So then, the weight of earth, its shape now formed,
Sank down;
And all the world sank down like slime or dregs of wine;
And then the sea and air in turn; aether in turn herself with flaming
                                                                    fires,
Were left unmixed like purest liquid when the dregs sink down.
(For each of these is lighter in successive steps.)
Aether, most liquid and most light,
Is borne along above air's breezes;
It mingles not at all with wind's tumultuous storms.
Aether allows the air below to churn in headlong hurricanes,
Or brawling shifting storms;
But aether, heedless of this,
Bears its fires along in changeless march.
The Black Sea gives a proof of this:
That sea which ever flows with changeless tide,
Yet ever keeps the even tenour of its way;

And so it proves that aether can flow serenely on,
In one great changeless tide.

Of stars

AND now the cause of motion and the stars I sing.
So, first of all, if Heaven's mighty orb revolves,
Then we must hold that air assails the pole at either end,
Constrains it from without and shuts it in on either side.
And then another stream of air flows on above
And strains to that same goal
To which the twinkling stars of everlasting universe eternally roll on.
Another stream below pushes the sphere with force reversed,
Just as we sometimes see the streams make mills revolve
With wheels and scoops.
Or it might be again,
That firmament of sky can stand unmoved,
Although the gleaming constellations move,
Either because swift surging streams of aether shut within the stars
Strive to escape and roll their fires this side and that
Throughout the nightly-thundering precincts of the sky.
Perhaps a gust of air from other quarters streams,
Pushes and turns the fires;
Perhaps the stars can creep themselves
Where food invites and tempts them as they move
To feed their flaming bodies everywhere in pastures of the sky.
To tell the cause in this our universe is hard.
But what can come to be and what does come to be
Throughout the whole,
In all the various worlds fashioned so differently,
Of this I teach,
Expounding various kinds of cause
Which might give motion to the stars throughout the whole.
One of these kinds of cause we know must by necessity

Give motion to the stars in our world too.
To say which one it is
Is not the task of one who treads his cautious way,
Makes headway step by step.
In order that the earth should rest
And hold the mid-place in the universe,
This is most natural
That earth should vanish bit by bit and lose its weight;
That it should have another substance underneath
Joined from its earliest day and made one unity
With those aethereal parts
To which it's grafted and with which it lives.
And so it proves no burden to the air, weighs it not down,
Just as his individual limbs are not a burden to a man;
Nor does his head weigh down his neck,
Nor does one feel the body's weight press heavy on one's feet.
But any burden placed on any man from the outside,
Will hurt, though smaller many times.
So crucial is it that we know the power that each thing has.
So then the earth is not brought in from foreign parts
In sudden rush;
Or from without is laid upon the wind—a foreign thing.
But with the wind the earth is shaped from first beginning of the
world,
And forms a fixed determined part of that
Like limbs and man.
Then, too, the earth when shaken by a violent thunder clap,
Shakes by its movement everything above.
And this it could not do
Were it not closely bound with airy parts of universe
And with the sky,
With common roots bound each to each they closely cling
From earliest times together bound and made one unity.

See, too, how soul—the thinnest, finest part of us,
Sustains the body with its mighty bulk.
Why? But so closely linked and made one unity?
Then too, what is there that could lift the body in a nimble leap
Except the soul which steers the limbs?
And now can you not see the power of unsubstantial things,
When linked with weighty matter
As air is linked to earth, and to our body mind?

The size of the sun and moon

Nor is the globe or heat of sun
Much larger or much smaller than they seem to human sense.
However great the distances through which the fires can hurl their
                                                                light
Or breathe soft warmth upon our limbs,
Yet in this interspace these fires lose nothing of their flames
They seem no smaller to our sight;
Just so the heat of sun, the light it sheds
Attack the organs of our sense,
And flood the place around with light;
It follows that the form and sight of sun are truly seen,
And nothing can you add or take away from that.
And whether moon with borrowed, bastard light,
Or with its own illumines all the world
(Whichever of these theories were the truth)
It's never larger than it seems to us.
Whatever at a distance we observe
These things are seen with outline all confused
Before their size is seen reduced.
And so the moon so clear in outline with such clear marked shape
Is seen by watchers on the earth
Just as she is on high,
With clear marked outline and no greater bulk.

And all the fires of heaven that from earth you see,
So long as blaze and twinkling of them seem clear,
Will alter only slightly in their size from time to time,
As they move off in space.
From this we know that only in an unimportant sense
Can these be larger, smaller than they seem to us.

The heat of the sun

NOR must we wonder that that tiny sun,
Can send so great a flood of light
To fill all seas and lands and sky with rose-red radiance,
Bathe them all in blazing heat.
Perhaps it's true that from this single spot
One bounteous source and fount of heat for all the world is opened
up,
That light abounds and pours illumination forth,
Because the particles of heat from all the world
From all sides come to meet and so pile up.
That from this single source derived
Their light and heat pour forth.
You've seen how o'er a wide expanse a tiny stream
Can irrigate the fields and flood the plain.
And sometimes too it comes about that though the fire of sun be small
The blazing sun takes hold of air in hot embrace,
If air is right and ready to be set alight
By blows of tiny rays of heat;
Just as we often see cornlands or heaps of straw
Blaze far and wide when kindled by a tiny spark.
This too could be
That sun, blazing aloft with rosy torch
Holds all around itself much fire with hidden heat—
But not revealed by any radiant light
And bringing with it surging tides of heat,

Adds to the force sent out by blazing rays of sun.
No simple tale, straightforward and direct was ever told
Of how the sun, leaving his summer haunts
Draws near the winter point of Capricorn,
And then returns to Cancer where he turns again;
Nor how in single months the moon
Can traverse all the yearly paths of sun.
No single cause, I say, is found for these.

Democritus' view of the sun

It may be as the splendid thought of that great Grecian seer Democritus proposed

The nearer are the stars to earth
The less they're whirled around by movements of the sky.
The powerful force of Heaven's whirl
Is scattered on its downward path;
Therefore the sun is left behind with rearward figures of the Zodiac
As lower far than fiery figures of the Zodiac;

The course of the moon

Much more the moon, the lower runs her course.
Farther from Heaven, nearer to the earth,
So much the less can she keep pace
With whirling constellations of the Zodiac.
Then too,
The weaker is the whirl by which the moon is borne along
(The moon you see is lower than the sun)
The more the various constellations in their various course
Can overtake the moon and pass her by.
And so the moon appears to make a swift return to all the con-
stellations of the sky,
Because the constellations seek the moon
More swiftly than they seek the sun.

It may be too, that at fixed times
A blast of air blows straight across the path of sun
Now from this side, now that
Which now can push the sun to Arctic cold and biting frost
And then again reverse, impel it to the realms of heat
And to the fiery figures of the Zodiac.
Likewise the moon and stars which move their mighty path
through mighty years
Are pushed now here, now there by varying blasts of air.
See too how lower clouds are borne along
In directions opposite to those above
By contrary winds;
Why not the stars by different winds
Through mighty circles in the sky?
Night overwhelms the earth in murky dark
Either when sun after its lengthy voyaging,
Has reached the furthest parts of sky;
Weak now and faint from travail of the road,
Weak too and faint from pressure of the endless air,
Has panted forth its heat;
Or else because the self same force
That drove the fiery orb along above the earth
Has made it turn its journey back below the earth.
Then too at the appointed time
The radiant deity of morn
Sends forth the rosy dawn throughout the shore of sky,
And spreads her light abroad.
Either because the self same sun, the sun you see
Returns again beneath the earth,
First makes himself the master of the sky,
And tries to kindle heaven with his rays.
Or, else because atomic particles of heat
Assemble in their multitude

And stream together at a certain time
And daily cause the light of sun to come again to birth.
On Ida's mountain height the legend tells
How scattered bits of flame were seen at dawn;
And then they seemed to coalesce, to form one ball.
And this should not seem wonderful
That particles of fire should stream together at a certain time,
Renew the splendour of the sun.
The bushes blossom at a certain time
And then again at certain times they lose their flowers.
The passing of the years at certain times
Makes teeth to fall.
At certain times the hairless youth
Begins to grow soft down,
The beard begins to fall down equally on either cheek.
And thunderbolts and snow and rains and clouds and winds
Occur at certain seasons of the year.
For since the origin of cause,
The orderly succession of events was ever thus,
And things have turned out so from first beginnings of the universe.
Even to day the order of events succeeds in due array.

The differing lengths of day and night

DAYS too grow long, nights fail,
Or nights grow long and strong while daylight dies
Either because that self same sun
As in unequal parts he takes his course above the world, below
Divides the shores of sky
And cuts his daily round into unequal parts;
And what he takes from one to the other he repays
As he goes round and round
Until he comes to that sign of the Zodiac
Where 'node of year' makes shades of night

And daylight balance equally.*
For when the path of sun
Holds place midway between the blasts from North and South
The sky sets turning posts apart to guide the chariot of the sun
At equal distance from the centre point
(The whole star-studded Zodiac
Through which the sun must creep, consume its yearly race
And light the lands and sky with slanting light,
Is placed just so.)
Of this for evidence we see the plans of those
Who map the wide expanse of sky and make a chart
Studded with all the constellations of the Zodiac.
Or else the reason is that air in certain parts of earth
Is more close-packed
And so the quivering ray of burning sun is held beneath the earth
And cannot easily pierce through, achieve the sunrise and the dawn.
And so in winter time the long nights linger on
Until, the radiant ensign of the day breaks forth.
Or else again because in varying seasons of the year
The fires which cause the sun to rise
From fixed and certain regions of the sky
Unite and stream together, sometimes slowly, sometimes fast.
And so it seems to me they speak the truth
Who say there is no single cause
For all the various movements of the sun.

On the light of the moon

WHERE smitten by the sun's bright rays the moon may shine
And daily more and more may turn her radiance to our sight,
The more she slips away from orb of sun;
And so when lady moon has found a place

* For an explanation of this difficult passage the reader should consult the SMITH-
LEONARD edition, p. 702.

Across the world from sun, she glows with fullest light
And as she rises, as she gains the heaven's peak,
She sees the setting of the sun.
And then again by stages imperceptible to us
She likewise must recede and hide her light,
The closer she approaches blazing light of sun,
Gliding from farthest side of sky
Through all the figures of the Zodiac.
As some imagine it who think the moon is like a ball,
And keeps the highway of her course beneath the path of sun.
This also might be true:
The moon might roll its own light round
And yet reveal its splendour in a great variety of forms.
It may be that another astral shape
Revolves through heaven together with the moon,
And blocks and blackens her at every turn,
And yet cannot be seen because devoid of light it journeys through
the sky.

Or moon may spin around like any ball
One half its surface dipped in gleaming light;
And as she turns reveal the various changing phases of the moon.
Until she shows to awestruck mortal sight and staring eyes
The side endowed with fire.
Then bit by bit she twists herself around again,
Removes from mortal sight the shining portion of the massive ball.
Chaldean sages long ago in Babylon
Put forth this explanation for the phases of the moon
And sought by this to overcome the scientific theories of astronomers.
And yet what each one holds and strives to prove may yet be true.
Nor need you venture to commit yourself
To this one theory, more or less than that.
Nor is there any reason why you should not hold
That every day a moon is made afresh, entirely new

With phases fixed in due array and foreordainéd shapes.
And so in several days the moon thus made might pass away,
Another be created in its room and place.
So hard it is to teach with reason's sovereign power,
Convince with words;
So many things can come to be in fixed array.

The succession of the seasons

Spring passes on its way and Venus, vernal god of spring.
Before them treads the love Queen's winged harbinger.
Hard on the footsteps of the South West wind
Flora the god of flowers holds wanton festival
And scatters all the road on which she treads
With splendid flowers before her dancing feet,
Yes and with glorious scents.
And after spring comes summer with its parching heat
Accompanied by the dusty goddess of the ripened grain,
And blasts of summer gales.
Then autumn stalks across the stage,
Who in her train brings revel rout,
The chant of Bacchic god.
And then the wild gales of the autumn equinox,
The east wind bringing thunders high aloft in sky,
The south wind glorious with the lightning's flash;
And then the end of every year brings snow and numbing torpid
                                                    cold and frost.
In winter's train comes chilling cold with chattering teeth.
And so it is not altogether wonderful
That moon be born at certain times,
At certain times again be blotted out;
Since all things come to be at certain times
In fixed array.

Eclipses

THEN too eclipses of the sun, concealment of the moon
For many reasons you must think might come to be.
For why could lady moon shut out the earth from light of sun
And push her head between him and the earth,
Blocking his radiant rays with dark, black orb,
Unless another heavenly form gliding eternally in everlasting dark
Could do the same?
Why could not father sun at fixed ordainéd time
Lose fire and faint and fail;
And then again renew its light,
Once, journeying through air,
He's passed the places hostile to his flames,
Places which dim and dull and doubt his fires?
And how could earth in turn rob moon of light,
And stand above the sun herself and hide his light
And in her monthly course pass through the sharp etched shadows
                                of the cone of light?
And yet another astral body could not pass beneath the moon
Or glide above the shining orb,
To break his gleaming rays and streaming light.
Yet none the less
If lady moon could shine with her own light
Why could she not grow faint and dim
In certain regions of the universe
The while she passes through the places hostile to her light?
Now for the rest since I have told
Through deep blue vault of mighty universe
The laws by which all things go on;
That now we've come to know the various courses of the sun and
                                moon
The power and cause that drives them on,
And what the cause that makes them hide, withhold their light,

And shadow unforseeing earth in unexpected shades of night,
When like a jovial man they wink, open the eye in turn
And look upon the world now bathed again in clear and shining
light.

Of early days on earth

Now I come back and tell of early days on earth,
And earth's soft fields;
And what the earth resolved in earliest pangs of birth
To bring to shining shores of light, entrust to gusty winds.
In early times, then, earth brought forth the varying kinds of grass
And foliage glowing green on all the hills around and over every
plain,
And flowery meadows flamed in radiance of green.
And then to various shrubs was given the power to leap into the air,
Like race horse on the track when reins are loosed.
And as on any fledgling four legged beast
Or strong winged bird of air,
Bristles and down and hair are formed,
So earth, new-born raised herbs and shrubbery first,
And then produced the tribes of living things—
Those various tribes that came to be
So variously in many ways.
For living creatures could not fall from sky,
Nor land born creatures leap from salty sea.
And so we must conclude that man was right
To call the earth his mother,
For from this mother earth were all things made.
Even today many creatures spring from earth,
Nurtured by rains and warming heat of sun.
And so it is not wonderful if when the earth was young and sky
was fresh

More creatures sprang from earth and larger creatures than the
                                            ones we know;
And, after birth, grew great and strong and reached maturity.
For first the wingéd fowl and all the birds
Emerged from eggs, were hatched in spring,
Even as now the grasshoppers
In summer leave their shapely shells spontaneously
To seek for life and livelihood.
And then the earth brought forth the mortal generations of all
                                            living things.
For in the early days of earth, moisture and heat abounded in the
                                            fields.
And thus wherever place seemed suitable, there sprang up female
                                            wombs
Which with their tentacles clung to the earth;
And when the time was fully ripe the tiny offsprings opened these
In flight from moisture and in search of air;
And where the tiny things appeared
Mother Nature turned the pores of earth
And from their open veins compelled a sap to flow
Most like the flow of milk.
Just as even now when women bring a child to birth
They fill with milk;
Because the pressure of their nourishment is turned towards the
                                            breasts.

And for these new-born tiny things
Earth gave forth food,
While warmth gave raiment
And the grass a bed, abounding with a wealth of soft and gentle
                                            down.

But earth was young and so did not produce
Hard frosts, excessive heat or over violent winds.
For all things grow alike, alike put on their strength.

And so again, I say, it's right,
That earth should gain and keep the name of Mother.
Since every creature—man and beast alike
She brings to birth—when time is ripe,
The beasts that revel everywhere on lofty hills,
And all the birds of air with all their varying forms.
But since it needs must be that earth should find
Some end to her creative work,
She ceased to bear like weary women at the menopause.
For time must change the nature of the universe—
A change of form and shape must come to everything
Nothing abides unchanged, all things must move.
Nature is always changing things
Compelling them to turn themselves around.
And one thing rots away, grows weak with age,
Another grows to take its place,
Leaving its former low estate.
So time must change the nature of the universe
A change of form and shape must come on everything;
And earth cannot now bear things that once it did,
Cannot bring to birth the things she once produced.
And many monsters in the early times
Earth strove to produce—
Creatures with curious face and limbs
Hermaphrodites like either sex,
But really neither sex, removed from both.
Or creatures without feet—sometimes lacking hands,
And speechless things that lacked a mouth,
Or sightless things that had no eyes,
Or things deformed with limbs unfree
So that they could accomplish not a single thing
Could move no where, avoid destruction or get sustenance.

And other monsters, other prodigies would mother nature bring
to birth.

Yet all in vain; they could not grow,
Attain the longed for flowering of their age, find sustenance,
Or join themselves in Venus' procreative task.
It needs must be that many factors coincide
Before a thing can reproduce its kind.
First they must have food;
And then there must be passages
Through which birth giving seeds may pass
And issue from their members now relaxed,
That female should be joined with male
And each exchange the common joys of mutual love.
It must have been that in the early days of earth
Countless kinds of living things died out
And failed to reproduce their kind.
For all the living things you now see feeding on the breath of life
Must have survived, after the first appearance of their kind,
Either through cunning or through valour or through speed of foot.
And many kinds have proved their usefulness to human kind,
Have lived and thrived
Because entrusted to the care of man.
The fierce and savage race of lions through valour has survived;
Foxes through cunning and the deer through speed.
But lightly sleeping loyal dogs,
The beasts of burden, fleecy flocks and hornéd kine
Are all, my friend, entrusted to the care of man.
Gladly they shunned the life of savage beasts
And sought domestic peace;
And bounteous fodder these have gained without the toil of raising
it—

The fodder which men give to various animals
To reward their usefulness to us.

To some has nature given neither way of life—
Survival by themselves spontaneously nor usefulness to man.
For which we let them live and feed, be safe, survive,
Under our kindly guardianship.
And these fell spoil and prey to other kinds
All caught in trammels of their luckless destiny
Until the time when nature had destroyed their race.

*Centaurs, Scylla the Chimaera and other fabled monsters could
never have come to be*

CENTAURS could never come to be
Nor creatures made of dual nature and a double shape,
Built up from members drawn from different kinds;
Their various parts could do no common task.
This we may know however dull our wits,
From this:
When three full years have passed a horse is in its prime,
But not a boy.
A boy at three will often blindly grope
For milky nipples of his mother's breasts,
But when the sturdy strength of steeds droops in old age
Their limbs begin to fail,
Manhood begins for boys at puberty,
And covers boyish cheeks with soft and downy beard.
And so you must not think that Centaurs could evolve or be
Formed from a man and burden bearing beast.
Nor could a Scylla come to be;
Creatures whose bodies are half fish
Girdled around by ravening dogs.
Nor any other creatures of this kind
Which men imagine made of parts from various kinds.
Parts which do not reach maturity at once,
Nor gain their strength at the same time,

Nor waste away together in the weakness of old age.
Nor do they flare with equal love
Nor are their habits like,
Nor will like food or comforts fit the various limbs throughout the
frame.

The bearded billy-goat will feed, grow fat on hemlock,
Which is deadly poison to a man.
And since a searing flame will scorch and burn
The tawny body of a lion,
Just as it scorches every kind of flesh
Who could believe chimaeras might be seen,
In front a lion, dragon behind, the middle part a goat
Breathing from its mouth a fierce flame?
A man who feigns that when the earth was young and sky new
born

Such creatures could arise,
(His only plea this silly argument—that earth was young)
Why such a man might babble anything.
He might pretend
That streams of gold flowed everywhere,
Trees were a bloom with precious stones,
That men were born with such expanse of limbs
That they could step across deep seas
Or twist the sky around with mighty strength of hands.
For though there were in earth
The countless seeds of countless things
When first the earth brought living creatures forth
This does not prove that beasts of mingled breed could come to be,
Or varying creatures joined in one.
Even today the grass, the crops, the fruitful trees,
Which spring abundantly from earth
Cannot be grafted so as to make a plant
With functions intertwined;

But in their several ways are each of these produced
And keep their several qualities by Nature's fixed unbending law.

Early days of the human race

THE human race was harder far in early days than now,
As you'd expect, since hard earth brought it forth.
Its bones within were harder, solider;
Its sinews binding flesh were tougher far.
Its hardy strength could hardly be assailed by heat or cold
Or novel food or any flaw in human frame.
Age after age while sun sped through the sky
They lived their life like wandering beasts.
No sturdy ploughman held his curving plough;
No skill was theirs to till the fields with iron share,
Or plant young shoots in earth,
Or prune high trees with knives.
The gift of sun and showers, spontaneous bounty of the earth,
Was boon enough to please their hearts.
Under the acorn-laden oaks they gained their sustenance;
Or dined on berried arbute
(These you've seen in winter red;
Much larger were they in the days of old.)
Besides all this the flowering youth of earth
Bore other fare as rough, plenty for wretched men.
To quench their thirst the rills and rivers called,
As now from mighty hills the water's fall
In loud and solemn tones calls thirsty roving beasts.
Or in their wandering they came to know
The woodland church of nymphs and lingered there.
For they knew
That water gliding there in bounteous flood
Washed the wet rocks and trickled over mosses green,
And sometimes welled and burst its banks

And rushed o'er level plain.
Not yet did man know how to serve himself with fire.
He had not thought to clothe himself with skins,
Use spoils of chase for body's covering.
Men dwelt in woods and glades and hollow mountain caves;
And hid their shaggy limbs in brushwood piles
When blows of wind or rain forced them to hide.
They could not think of social good
Or know the fine restraint of common codes or laws.
Whatever booty fortune gave the individual seized
His only learning was to live and thrive himself.
Venus herself joined lovers in the woods in primal ecstasy.
Sometimes a mutual love joined man and girl
Or else the violent strength of male, unbridled lust.
Or else she was by little gifts seduced—
Acorn or arbute or the choicest pear.
Relying on their wondrous strength of hand and foot
Men followed hard on track of woodland beasts,
With mighty clubs or stones to hurl.
Most they subdued, a few they'd dodge and hide.
When night came on they laid their naked limbs on earth
Like bristling boars,
And wrapped themselves around with leaves and foliage.
Nor did they look for day light and the sun with wailing loud,
Or wander panicked through the fields at black of night;
But deep in silent sleep they waited patiently
Till sun with rosy torch brought light to sky.
For since from babyhood they'd learned to know
Light following darkness, turn by turn, and darkness light,
They had no sense of wonder or of fear,
No sense of apprehension lest the sun should ne'er return,
And earth be buried always in unending night.
Their fear was rather this, that savage beasts

Might make night restless for a wretched folk.
They left their homes, abandoned rocky roof
If foaming boar or mighty lion approached.
At midnight oft they'd leave their leaf spread couch
To savage and unwelcome guests.
And not much more in early times than now
Did men lament to meet untimely end
And leave the sweet bright light of life behind.
Sometimes a hapless man in earliest times
Was caught by savage beasts,
Ground by their teeth and gulped down ravenously.
The woods and glades and hills he'd fill with piteous cries
Aghast while living flesh was buried in a living tomb.
But some escaped by flight though mangled, torn and maimed.
And these then held their trembling hands
Over their awful sores
And piteous in their anguished cries would beg release,
Until in ignorance of how to dress the wounds
The cramping, griping pains brought death.

But in remote antiquity men could escape
the wholesale slaughter of our modern days

But in remote antiquity men could escape
The wholesale slaughter of our modern days.
Never were thousands at a time enrolled in warlike hosts
By thousands in a single day to meet catastrophe.
Nor were great liners with their complements of passengers and
crew
Dashed on the rocks in early days.
The sea would often rise and rage,
But idly, rashly, vainly would it roar,
And then lay down its idle, empty threats in turn;

No man was coaxed to death
By winning guileful smile of windless wave.
The treacherous art of navigation was as yet unknown.
In ancient times the lack of food brought men to death;
Now over abundance lays them low.
Those ancient savages in ignorance poisoned themselves;
But now with knowledge, forethought, skill,
Men hand the poisoned cup to their associates.

Origin of the family

AND when as time went on, men came to master fire,
Gained themselves huts and skins to cover them,
One man, one woman in a single hut together lived,
And tiny ones around them growing up they saw,
Then first the human race learned gentler ways.
Now used to fire
Their freezing limbs would shrink from cold beneath the vault of
sky.

Excessive sex wore down their savage strength,
And children with their blandishments
Subdued their elder's haughty will.
Then neighbour oft to neighbour pledged his word
Eager to form a friendship and refrain from mutual harm.
And pity they'd evoke for girls and children, too,
When these with piteous cries,
Pathetic gestures and the broken word
Would teach the primal law of moral life
That all should spare the weak.
Yet concord was a lesson hard to learn.
Most of mankind was loyal to its pledge.
Else would the human race in earliest times have failed
Nor wealth of progeny sufficed destruction to avert.

NATURE compelled our early ancestors to utter various sounds,
And use worked out the names of things.
Just as you see with children growing up:
Their very speechlessness
Compels them to gesture, with their fingers point
At things before their eyes.
For every creature knows instinctively
The ends to which to turn its innate powers.
A calf will butt and use his forehead angrily,
Long before horns appear.
The young of panthers and of lions
Will bite and scratch and tear
When claws and teeth are scarcely formed.
Birds too we see trusting their sprouting wings
Getting from these a wavering, wobbly kind of help.
And so to think that someone summoned everything,
Assigned a name to each,
To think that men have learned from him the names of things
Is foolishness, my friend.
How could this first inventive man
Mark off the names of everything,
Give out the sounds of vocal utterance—
A thing which no contemporary could do?
If others had not uttered speech, communicating thought
How did he get the notion of its use?
And whence was given to him this early power
To know, imagine in his mind just what he wished to do?
Nor could one man keep many down, compel them to his will,
And make them learn the names he'd given to things.
(You know yourself it is not easy to persuade and teach the deaf
What they should do;
The deaf would not put up with you,

Would not allow the sounds of words not understood
To batter at their ears so long in vain.)
And if the human race, with voice and tongue so strong,
Should for diverse emotions utter different sounds,
What is so wonderful in this?
Even domesticated beasts who've never learned to speak,
Even wild beasts give out a different noise,
When fear or pain or joy grow strong within.
This we can learn from things easy to see.
When the large, loose, pulpy lips of hounds—
Molossian hounds—
In anger snarl, the dogs lay bare their hard white teeth,
With lips drawn back they snarl and make a threatening noise
Quite different from the noise they make
When they just bark and fill the place around with sound.
Quite different too the noise they make
When fondlingly they lick their puppies with their tongues
Or toss them with their feet,
Or make for them with open mouths
Gently pretend to swallow them but check their teeth
And fondle them with growling voice.
Quite different is the noise they make when left alone
In some deserted house and bay;
Quite different, too, the noise they make
If you should try to beat them and they crouch
And whimper and avoid your blows.
Or think again:
When a young stallion in the flower of youth and youthful years
Rages among the mares,
Pricked by the spur of wingéd love
Does he not make a very different neigh
Than when with nostrils spread he snorts for war
Or when he whinnies a tremble in his limbs?

Then, too, the tribes of wingéd things, the different birds,
The hawks and ospreys and the pale grey gulls
That seek their life and living on the ocean's salty waves
Give out at times quite different sounds than those they make
Fighting for food and struggling with their prey.
Some birds can change their notes as seasons change.
The flocks of long-lived crows and rooks are said to croak for rain,
Summon the wind with different cries at other times.
And so if voiceless creatures are constrained
By different feelings to give out a different sound,
How much more likely is it that the human race
Could give to different things a different name?

Origin of fire

HERE I'll anticipate your silent questionings.
'Twas lightning's flash that first brought fire to man,
And from that source all heat of flame is spread abroad.
Even to this day we see that many things burst into flame,
Sparked by the fire from heaven
When heaven's blow has brought the gift of heat.
Again, when branching tree is lashed by winds,
Sways to and fro and surges with its boughs against another tree.
Fire often flashes forth,
Induced by friction of a bough on bough.
In either way fire may have come to man.
The sun taught men to cook their food,
To soften it with heat of flame;
So many things they saw grow mellow in the fields,
Quite beaten by the blows and heat of sun.
And men pre-eminent for intellect and strength of mind,
Would daily show their fellows how to change their ways,
Adapt themselves to novelty and fire.

Now kings began to lay out cities and to choose
Sites for their citadels, to give protection to their persons
And a place of refuge.
And flocks and herds and fields were parcelled out
As individual holdings,
Given to men pre-eminent in bearing, talent, strength,
(For comeliness was vital then, strength of physique prevailed)
Then came a fell invention, property, the power of gold.
This undermined the power of strong and noble men.
The faction of the rich quite generally,
Sucks in a man though strong and nobly born.
So, if a man would guide his life aright by reason's principles,
Plain living with a mind at peace is wealth indeed.
The little that he needs man never lacks.
But men have longed for wealth and power pre-eminent,
To build a strong foundation under life,
That wealth enable them to lead a life of quiet tranquillity,
But all in vain.
While mad to scale the dizzy heights of honour and of fame
They've made the path of life with dangers teem.
Often they think their striving's reached the peak,
But envy, like a thunderbolt,
Has hurled them down to noisome depths.
Since envy like a lightning flash
Sets topmost heights ablaze,
Whatever is pre-eminent most generally.
Better to be a subject with a mind at peace
Than hold the kingdom's power and kingly sway.
Permit men, then, to sweat away the blood of life,
Worn out in vain;
Fight their way forward on ambition's narrow way.
Vain is the wisdom gained from lips of other men,

Vain fantasy by hearsay, not experience, won.
Such spurious unsight cannot help mankind.
It never has, it never will.

And so the kings were killed

AND so the kings were killed,
The ancient prideful majesty
Of thrones and sceptres trampled down.
The glorious majesty that hedged a king was stained with blood,
Crushed 'neath the people's feet,
And mourned its ancient high estate, now lost.
The object once of fear, it now in squalor lies.
The ancient polity, I say, is trampled down.
Each single man, self-centred now
Plays his own hand, seeks gain for self alone.
To check all this,
The cleverer men established magistrates
And founded laws that subject folk might willingly obey.
The human race, wearied with passing life in mutual violence,
Lay faint from feuding.
And so spontaneously it would submit to statutes
And the woven web of laws.
Because each single man sought vengeance for himself
More savage than allowed by equal laws,
On this account they tired of mutual retribution.
And so it comes about that fear of punishment
Has come to spoil and spatter every joy of life.
His individual deeds of violence hem a man in,
Returning like a boomerang on him from whom they sprang.
Nor can he pass his life in peace and quietness,
If once his deeds of violence
Break through the common accepted pacts of peace.
And even if he hides his sins from all mankind, all gods,

Still lurks the fear that some day they'll be known.
Often a man by talking in his sleep or raving in delirium
Has bared an ancient crime which he'd kept hidden long.

Origin of belief in the gods

AND now the cause
That spread belief in deity through mighty folk,
And filled our towns with shrines,
And prompted men to institute the rites of solemn sacrifice,
Which linger even to this day on festal days and in great places
(Whence, even now, horror is branded in our human hearts,
Compelling men to found new shrines of gods and celebrate
On festal days),
All this it's not so hard to tell in words.
Even in ancient times the human race
Perceived with waking eyes the glorious shape of gods;
Much more in sleep, they thought they saw
Bodies of supernatural size and form.
To forms like these was consciousness assigned
Because men saw them move their limbs,
Utter proud words proportionate to their size and mighty strength.
Immortal life men gave to them,
Because their face appeared from time to time,
Their form remained.
But most of all because they thought
That creatures blest with strength like this
Could not be overcome by any force.
They thought their lot must better be than ours
Because no fear of death could harass them.
And, too, because in dreams they could perform
Many miraculous deeds in manner effortless.
And then men marked in due array the ordered laws of sky,
The splendid pageant of the seasons of the year,

But did not know the cause.
And so they sought escape,
By handing all things over to divine control,
By thinking all things ruled by god's decree.
They placed the temples and abodes of gods above the sky
Because the sun and moon revolved through sky,
The moon and day and night,
The splendid stars of night,
Night-wandering torches and the flitting flames,
And clouds and sun and showers and snow and winds,
Lightnings and hail and rapid thunder claps,
Those turbulent, tremendous threats.
O hapless race of men,
When deeds like this to gods assigned
Were joined to petty vengefulness!
What groans for you, what wounds for us,
What tears for later ages.
This is not holiness, before the sight of men,
Day after day to crawl up to a stone
(The ritual veil on head)
And never miss an altar;
Nor prostrate lie before the shrines of gods with outstretched palms
Nor slaughter hecatomb on hecatomb,
Nor weave a litany of vow on vow.
No. Holiness is this: to contemplate with mind serene the whole.
When we lift eyes to great celestial temples of the world,
Aether above, studded with twinkling stars,
And let thoughts roam on heaven's immensity,
The ordered course of sun and moon and stars,
Then this reflection starts to stir and wake and raise its head,
That this tremendous power of god might turn on us,
This power that moves the constellations
In their endless, restless way.

The lack of scientific thought assails the doubting heart,
No knowledge how the cosmos came to be and how 'twill end,
How long the ramparts of the universe
Can bear the task of endless, restless journeying,
Or whether, gifted by divine decree with endless life,
And gliding endless down the grooves of time,
They can defy the strength of time's eternity.
And, after all,
What mind escapes the sudden flash of fear, fear of the gods,
When lightning's dreadful stroke,
Makes parched earth tremble and the great sky crash?
Nations and peoples tremble,
Shrink and huddle limbs together out of fear, terror of gods,
The thought that now's the time
For some foul deed, for some proud word,
To suffer retribution's torment.
Or when the force of furious wind at sea
Sweeps fleet and admiral and horse and foot in headlong rout,
Does he not beg in prayer the peace of god,
That heaven will bless with calmer seas and favouring winds?
But all in vain, for nonetheless,
He's caught in whirling hurricanes and helpless borne
To shallow waters and to death.
A mighty hidden force so tramples down
All human strength,
Treads under foot and seems to hold in mockery
The pomp of power and power's relentless instruments,
The savage axes and the lovely rods.
Again, when all of earth trembles beneath our feet,
Cities are shaken to their fall
Or threatening rock and quake,
What wonder that mankind contemns itself
And leaves place in its thought

238

For mighty power and marvellous strength of god
To govern all things?

The discovery of minerals

Now for the rest:
Copper and gold and iron were found,
The weight of silver and the usefulness of lead,
When fire had ranged through mighty hills
And burnt a vast extent of forest land;—
Either when the lightning flash from sky had set the woods ablaze
Or when the tribes were waging war through forest glades
And set the woods afire to frighten and dismay their enemies;
Or else, because enchanted by the richness of the land,
They wished to clear the fertile fields,
To make a pasture of the country side;
Or else they wished to put the game to death,
Enrich themselves with booty of the chase.
(Hunting with pit or flames developed long before
Men learned to fence the grove with nets
Or scare their game with dogs.)
However that may be,
Whatever caused the flaming heat to eat away the woods from deep-
                                                        est roots,
(The woodlands crack and crash the while most dreadfully)
And bake the earth,
Then streams of gold and silver, copper and lead
Trickled from the boiling veins
And gathered in the hollow places on the ground.
And when primaeval man had seen these nuggets afterwards
With brilliant colour, hard and shining on the ground,
Charmed by their beauty and their smoothness they would pick them
                                                        up,

And notice how their shape was moulded by the shape of earth's
contours.
And then a thought came creeping in their minds.
Perhaps these metals might be melted by the heat
And take the form or shape of anything.—
Be shaped and hammered out to form the sharp fine tips and points
Of arrows and of spears;
That so they might make weapons for themselves and tools;
That with these tools they might fell forest trees,
Hew timbers, plane beams smooth,
And bore and punch, drill holes.
At first they tried to do just this with silver and with gold
Just as much as with stout copper's sturdy penetrating strength.
But all in vain of course.
The power of gold and silver had to yield,
Nor equally with copper could they bear the cruel toil.
And in those days copper was valued, gold despised as useless,
Too soon blunted in its poor, dull edge.
But in our days the opposite is true.
Gold is most highly valued, copper is despised.
Just so the rolling series of the centuries
Changes men's estimates of things.
What once was valued finds neglect in turn,
What once despised is daily more esteemed,
Bursts into sudden blaze of flame.
How iron was found, my Memmius,
You yourself can learn quite easily.
Men used as weapons in the days of old
Their hands and nails and teeth;
Then stones; and branches torn from forest trees;
Then later fire and flame when fire was known.
Then after that was found the power of iron and bronze—
Bronze before iron;

For bronze is easier to work and comes in greater quantities.
With bronze men worked the soil;
With bronze they mingled waves of war, dealt out great wounds,
And seized both flocks and fields.
No wonder:
Men unarmed and naked had to yield to those who carried arms.
Then bit by bit the iron sword made its way,
The brazen sickle came to be despised.
With iron men ploughed the soil.

Development of weapons of war

THE use of weapons evened up the tides of dubious war.
And long before with chariot and with horses yoked
Men faced war's perilous opportunities,
They'd come to mount in full array a fiery horse,
To guide the horse with reins,
And deeds of valour do with strong right arms.
Men learned to yoke two horses to a chariot much before four,
And climb in full array into a car equipped with scythes.
The men of Carthage taught the elephant—
The frightful elephant with turrets on its back,
Grim beasts with snaky hands,
To bear the wounds of war,
And throw confusion through a mighty martial host.
And so grim Discord brings to pass thing after thing,
To plague and panic men at arms;
And day by day Discord increased the terrors and the fear of war.
Other devices men have tried in striving for the victory in war.
Bulls they have launched against the foe or savage boars.
Some have sent before their marshalled host
A screen of raging lions,
Schooled by armed teachers, savage pedagogues,
To keep them in control, bind them in chains,

But this device was all in vain.
The lions' hearts grew hot in th' confused affray;
Tossing their tawny, awful manes they charged
The squadrons of the cavalry—both sides alike.
Nor could the horsemen sooth their frightened mounts,
Nor with their bridles make them face the foe.
The maddened lions seemed to leap on every side,
And hurl themselves against the faces of their adversaries,
Or catch them in unguarded moments from behind;
Then faint as they were from wounds the savage beasts
Twisted and threw them to the earth,
And gripped them with their curving claws and powerful bite.
Bulls too would turn and rend their masters and their friends,
Gash with their horns the flanks and bellies of the horses under-
                                                                neath,
And snort and stamp and rage and paw the ground.
The wild boars too with strong and savage tusks
Slew their allies.
The weapons hurled at them would break,
Lodged in the bull's tough hide,
(The boar's own red blood would stain the spears)
While horse and foot fell tangled to the ground,
Tangled in one fell heap.
Horses would swerve in order to escape the savage teeth,
Or rear and beat the air with frightened feet,
But all in vain;
With tendons severed they would fall
And in their headlong crash would strew the ground.
Men thought to tame the creatures in advance—
Thought they were tame enough to do their will
But in the heat of battle's clash
Fury burst forth in creatures maddened by the wounds, the shouts,
                                                        the panic, flight.

Confusion raged through all the ranks;
Nor could the soldiers rally any of their beasts.
The various kinds would scatter, hither and yon.
Even as now the elephants cruelly mangled by the steel
Scattering in headlong rush
Bring deadly harm and peril to their friends.
If indeed men really acted so.
But for my part I can scarce believe
That men would not imagine in advance what the result would be
If humankind gave all its mind to this grim task
Of bringing to perfection all the arts of war.
Perhaps this picture of warfare's development
Is what might happen in the various worlds that make our universe
Rather than what occurred in any one.
Perhaps men did all this
Not so much in hopes of victory
But despairing of themselves and of their cause
Outmatched in numbers, lacking arms,
They thought to give their foemen cause to mourn,
While going up themselves in one transcendent, glorious suicide.

Origin of clothing

LONG before the woven cloth was known
Men learned to plait their clothes.
To weave a cloth came late—well after iron was found.
From iron the loom was made and must be made;
From nothing else can treadles smooth be formed
Spindles or, shuttles or the sounding rods.
And males by nature's ordering worked wool,
Long before women learned the art;
(For men have more of skill and knowledge too.)
Until the sturdy ploughman came to scorn these arts,
Content to leave them to a woman's hands,

While they were glad themselves to bear hard toil,
And with the day's hard grind to harden hands and limbs.

Origin and development of agriculture

NATURE herself, creative Queen of everything,
Gave men a pattern how to sow and graft.
Berries and nuts would fall from trees,
And then, when time was ripe, put out their shoots in swarms.
From Nature, too, men learned to graft a wand to parent stem,
Plant shrubs in soil.
And various ways they learned to till their smiling fields
Domesticate both fruits and beasts
By care and constant tending.
And day by day they beat the woodland back,
Back up the mountain slopes and made the valleys yield a place for
crops.
That so they might on hill and plain
Have meadows, pools and streams,
Corn lands and vineyards that bring joy to men,
And grey-green belts of olive trees
Checkering the landscape over hill and vale and plain.
As even now you see the country side
Made beautiful with various charms,
Where men have made it gay by planting trees,
And fenced it in around with fruitful shrubs.

Origin of music

To imitate the liquid notes of birds
Men learned long, long ago,
And much before he'd learned to sing in company sweet songs,
To entrance the ear.
The west wind whistling through the hollow reeds
First taught the country folk to breathe through scrannel pipes.

244

Then bit by bit they learned the sweet lament—
The elegies that flutes poured forth,
Their holes by fingers stopped.
Through pathless glades the sweet sound made its way
And forest deeps, through fields by shepherds left,
And lovely resting place.
So bit by bit time brings each thing to view,
And reason raises it to shores of light.
These tunes would soothe their minds, delight their ears,
When they lay stuffed with food.
(That's when all pleasure brings delight.)
For often, as we've said, in grassy nook reclined
A stream a shady tree instead of luxury,
With no great wealth they tend the body's needs,
And find sufficient bliss
Spring on the mountains, flowers in every meed.
Then you'd hear jokes and talk and pleasant laughs
(The rustic muse was strong),
And life was gay and mirth made garlands for their heads
Of flowers and leaves.
And round they'd dance
With random step and clumsy limbs.
With heavy foot their rhythmic tread would beat on mother earth.
This made them laugh in merry mood.
All things, like children, in the childhood of the race,
They found both strange and new.
So to the wakeful came the solace of sweet sounds,
To guide the erring voice through many a tune,
Follow the endless windings of a song,
To pipe on reeds with curling lips.
Even today
Policemen and sentries hold this old tradition fast,
Have learned to keep the rhythm of a song,

But find therein no greater bliss
Than woodland folk of earth-born men
Found long ago.
For what is here and now pleases men most, seems best,
Unless there's something sweeter that we've learned of old.
But generally
The better thing found later on destroys the old.
And makes us like it less.
And so it is
That man has come to like his fare of acorns less,
Abhor his reed-strewn couch.

On fashion

GARMENTS of skins, no longer fashion's peak,
Were envied long ago.
The first to sport such luxury, I think,
Was ambushed, slugged and put to death,
And yet in killing him
They tore the coat apart, stained it with blood,
And could not sell for gain.
Of old 'twas skins.
Now gold and purple vex men's lives with care
And weary them with constant, endless wars.
We are to blame, I think.
Cold used to torture earth born men
As they lay naked on the earth without the warmth of pelts.
But we're not harmed without our purple cloth,
With massive golden ornament.
We only need a poor man's cloak to keep out cold.
And so the race of men toils endlessly, in vain.
It wastes its time in fruitless cares
Because, it's never learned the end of gain
And how far pleasure true can go.

And this has drawn life's ship to stormy seas,
Stirred up great tides of war.

The watchful wardens of the firmament, the moon and sun.
Traversing with their light the whirling vault of sky,
Taught men that seasons of the year revolve,
That all things move by some fixed plan,
In fixed and due array.
And now fenced in with mighty walled towns
Man lived his life.
The land was parcelled out in plots and fenced and tilled.
Then ocean's level wastes bloomed with the sails of ships.
Men learned to make a compact,
Seal a bond between allies for mutual aid;
Then poets first began to sing immortal deeds in glorious verse.
(The alphabet was new when poets sang.)
Therefore our age knows nothing of the past,
Except where science points out the scattered bits of evidence.
And so man made his way.
Experience, the tireless search of eager mind,
Has taught him many things—
Of ships and walls and laws, weapons and roads,
Of how to till the soil and how to dress;
And all life's prizes, life's delights,
Pictures and songs and statues finely wrought.
He's learned them stage by stage and bit by bit.
So step by step time brings each thing to view
And reason raises it to shores of light.
Thing after thing grew clear in human hearts
Until man's art assailed perfection's peak.

Book Six

In praise of Epicurus

IN DAYS OF OLD
'Twas Athens, Cecrops' town, of glorious memory
That first gave fruitful crops of grain to wretched men,
And fashioned human life afresh
And laid down laws.
And Athens, too, first gave to mortal men sweet solaces
By giving birth to that great man,
Gifted with mighty intellect,
Who once poured forth the deep thoughts of philosophy,
From lips that always told the truth;
Whose glory, even when the light of life was quenched
Noised abroad of old
Is now made equal to the sky.
For when he saw that man had everything
Which nature really needs for human life,
Existence for the human race as far as possible assured,
And men exulting in their power,
With wealth and honours and renown
Proud of the reputation of their young;
Their hearts at home were no less anxious in spite of reason
And care harassed their lives
And made them moan aloud in dire complaint;

He came to see
That fundamental fault lay with the human vase,
That its corruption tainted all the mind and soul within,
Corrupted all that came within the case from outer life,
Even life's best rewards.
Partly because the vase was cracked and full of holes,
And never could be filled,
Partly because its evil taste corrupted everything within.
And so with words of truth he purged the human heart,
He set a limit to desire and fear,
Described the highest good for which all humans strive,
And pointed out the straight and narrow path
By which we reach the highest good.
The various forms of evil flitting everywhere through human life
Produced through natural chance or Nature's laws,
(If Nature thus ordained or willed)
All this he showed;
And also how to raise the siege against the foul array
And from which gates the beleaguered self should issue forth and
fight.

He proved that all in vain
Mankind allowed the gloomy waves of care to toss and roll within the
heart.

Like tiny boys who tremble in the dark
And think that anything may come,
We also tremble in the light
And shrink from things that in themselves are no more terrible
Than what boys fear in dreams and fancy sure to be.
And so this darkened terror of the mind must be dispelled
Not by the rays of, sun or gleaming shafts of day
But Nature's laws, by looking in her face.
Now since I've shown the universe to be made of mortal stuff
The heavens created out of matter that was born in time,

Unravelling almost all that happens in the universe,
And what must come to pass
Now hear the rest.
Now since I've entered once for all
The viewless chariot of poesy, I'll venture to explain
How raging storms of winds arise and how they are appeased,
And how all things find peace again
When raging of the storm is stilled.
And all the things which men observe
To happen on the earth and in the sky,
And often hang upon events with panic-stricken minds,
And grovel in their intellects through fear of gods
And huddle puppyish minds to earth,
Because in ignorance of what has really caused the happening
They feel compelled to hand it over to divine dominion
Admit the power of gods.
For even men who've fully learned that gods lead care-free lives,
If ignorant of laws by which things move,
Those things in chief which happen overhead, up in the sky,
They're drawn to ancient creed and cult again,
Imagine savage tyrants overhead, strong to accomplish anything;
Because, poor fools, they know not what can come to be and what
cannot,
The law that binds each thing, its deep set boundary stone.
And so they wander here and there in mind's blind blundering.
Unless you spit all thoughts like these away from you,
And shun to think of things unworthy of the gods,
Unworthy of their peace,
The holy power of gods degraded by your thought
Will often do you harm.
I do not mean that heaven's awful majesty
Can really be assailed by any thought of yours,
And long to visit you with savage punishment;

Rather that you yourself might think
These tranquil beings in their long untroubled peace
Might set in motion mighty waves of wrath.
And then you won't approach the holy shrines of gods
With hearts at peace
Nor be strong to take into your mind,
Like theirs at peace,
Those holy visions of the sacred form of god
That show the shape of godhead to the minds of men.
And you yourself must know,
How far removed from sweet tranquillity
That life would be.
In order, then, that true philosophy
May keep you far from such a life as this,

His task in this book

ALTHOUGH I've said a lot, yet much remains to say, expound and orna-
ment,
With polished verse.
For grasp we must the inner workings of the earth and sky.
My song must tell of storm and blinding lightning flash,
Both what they do and how they're caused,
So will you not in deep anxiety
Survey like Tuscan soothsayers the various quarters of the heaven
and ask
Whence came this fleeting flash?
Where did it go?
How did it penetrate through walls,
And leave again after its moment's mastery of the house.
Men see no cause for happenings like this
And think they happen by divine decree.
Do thou, O clever Muse Calliope,
Repose of men, delight of gods,

Mark out for me the track,
As now I speed towards the white chalk line
That marks the goal.
With you to guide I'll gain the victor's wreath,
While all humanity applauds.

Meteorological phenomena: a) Thunder

FIRST then the blue expanse of sky is shaken by a thunder clap,
Because the clouds aloft that scud across the vault of heaven
Meet and clash wherever wind contends with wind.
Not from a sky serene does thunder crack,
Rather when clouds are massed in dense array
Thence comes the sullen roar and mighty rumbling.
And yet the clouds are not as dense as sticks or stones,
Nor yet so thin as mists or eddying smoke;
For were they dense like sticks and stones
The clouds would fall, dragged by their own dead weight
And were they thin like smoke
They could not hold and keep aloft chill snow or showers of hail.
And clouds give out a crack
Over the levels of the spreading firmament
As sometimes canvas spread over a mighty theatre gives a crack,
While tossing madly 'tween the masts and beams.
Sometimes the canvas revels wild, torn by the raging winds
And makes a noise like sheets of paper when they're torn.
(You've often heard a sound like that in thunder claps);
Or else a second noise,
Like that which hanging garments makes
Or whirling papers when they're tossed and buffeted
By raging winds.
Sometimes it happens too,
That clouds do not meet face to face in head on clash,
But as they move from different sides

252

Just graze obliquely, flank on flank,
Their bodies grate;
And then a dry and crackling sound and long drawn out
Assails the ears,
Until the clouds escape their narrow prisoning space.
In this way too,
The mighty total universe often seems to quake
When smitten by a heavy thunder clap;
The mighty ramparts of the all-embracing universe
Are torn, it seems, and leap apart,
When suddenly a gathered storm of mighty wind
Has forced its way into the clouds.
Imprisoned there, its whirling eddy hollows out increasingly the
                                                                    cloud,
And makes the enclosing vapor dense on every side;
Until the cloud is weakened by the impetuous onslaught of the wind,
It splits and makes a rending crash
With frightening, threatening sound.
That's not so strange when even a little bladder filled with air,
Gives out a little noise when bladder bursts.
Or this cause might explain how it could be
That when winds blow through clouds they make a din.
Often we see clouds borne along, branching out in many ways,
Rough at the edge;
Just as when the North West wind is blowing through a dense thick
                                                                    wood.

The leaves give out a noise, the boughs a rending crash.
Sometimes the impetuous onslaught of a powerful wind
Tears through a cloud and breaks it up
By a direct attack.
Now what the blast can do on high
Is shown by things we often see on earth.
For though the wind is gentler here

It often tears a mighty tree out by the roots
And sucks it up on high.
Waves, too, move through the clouds
Which make a mighty noise
Like waves of water breaking on the coast.
It happens on deep rivers and the mighty sea
When surf breaks on the shore.
This happens too when fiery force of thunderbolts
Is passed from cloud to cloud.
If it should happen that the cloud receives the flame in wet embrace,
It straightway ends its life in mighty noise.
Just as a piece of iron when white from furnace heat
Will hiss if quickly plunged in water cold.
But if a drier cloud receives the flame
It catches fire at once and burns with dreadful noise.
Just as if a fire broke out on laurel crested hills
And roamed abroad, whipped by the eddying winds,
And burned the laurels as it passed.
(For nothing sounds so fearful, as it burns
As Delphic laurel that Apollo loves.)
Then too the bounteous crack of ice,
The fall of hail,
Will often make a noise in clouds on high.
For when the wind has packed them in a narrow space
Mountains of cloud, congealed and mixed with hail,
Explode.

Meteorological phenomena: b) Lightning

LIKEWISE will lightning flash when clashing clouds strike out
The seeds of fire in multitude.
Just as if stone should strike on stone
Or iron on iron.
Then too a flame flares out and scatters brilliant sparks.

We hear the thunder with our ears long after eyes have seen the
lightning flash,
Because sensations strike the ear,
Much later than they strike the eye.
And this example will convince you of the truth of this;
If you watch men afar who fell a tree with double bladed axe
You see the stroke,
Much earlier than the sound of it assails the ear.
And so we see the lightning long before we hear the thunder clap,
Though both set out together on their way,
With cause the same, and born from the same clash.
In this way too,
The clouds will colour places on the earth beneath
With leaping light.
The storm will light the earth with quivering attack.
When wind has entered in the cloud and whirled about
And made the hollow cloud grow dense;
Its own swift movement makes it hot.
All things grow hot from movement and catch fire.
A ball of lead if whirled for long will melt.
And so when this hot wind has torn black clouds apart
It scatters far and wide the seeds of fire,
As though by violence suddenly hurled forth
Which make the quivering flash of flame.
Then comes the sound, later the sound assails our ears,
Then things which reach the vision of our eyes.
This you must know occurs in thick dense clouds
In clouds heaped up in wondrous massive piles.
(You must not be deceived because, standing below,
We sense the breadth of things and not their height.)
Come, look yourself:
Next time the winds bear clouds through air like mountain shapes,

When next you see the massive clouds piled high on mighty moun-
tain range,
Pressing each on each,
Each finding rest in its own proper place;
When winds on every side are buried in their graves.
Then you can see their mighty mass—
The caverned clouds with vaulted roofs,
And when the storm arises,
And winds have filled the cloudy caves,
These winds imprisoned in the clouds will chafe,
With threatening roar,
Like savage beasts imprisoned in a cage.
Now here, now there they send their fury through the clouds,
And move round restlessly to find escape,
And roll the seeds of fire from out the clouds,
And so collect them in their multitude,
Roll them around within the hollow furnace of the cloud;
Until the cloud is burst
And shimmering winds rush out like tongues of flame.
For this cause, too
The swift and golden blaze of liquid fire
Swoops down to earth—
Because the clouds themselves have many seeds of fire
(When clouds are altogether dry)
Their colours like to bright and splendid flame.
For many seeds of fire they catch,
The seeds that stream from sun itself;
No wonder then they glow and pour forth fire.
When, then, the winds have driven them,
And pushed and packed them in one spot,
They squeeze and pour abroad the seeds of flame which make the
fires flash out.
But lightning can flare, too, when clouds grow thin.

For when the wind with lightest touch draws moving clouds apart,
And breaks them up,
The seeds which make the lightning flare fall out themselves.
But then the flash is not accompanied by obscene tumult, panic or
noise.

Meteorological phenomena: c) Thunderbolts

THE nature of the thunderbolt is shown by marks it makes,
By indications branded by its heat—
The hollows breathing noisome sulphur smoke,
All these are marks of fire and not of wind or rain.
Then too they often set the roofs afire;
The licking tongues of flame hold sway within the house itself.
This lightning fire, you know,
Is made by nature subtle, fine
Finer than other tiny, nimble atom shapes;
This nothing in the world can stop.
The sturdy thunderbolt can penetrate through dwellings, walls,
Just as can shouts and cries;
It goes through rocks, through objects made of bronze,
And in a twinkling it liquefies both bronze and gold.
It makes the wine evaporate—and suddenly,
Though bottles are untouched;
Because its heat in striking all around
Makes porous, loosens up the porcelain of the vase,
And swiftly makes its way within the wine,
Dissolves, breaks up its atom stuff.
Yet this the heat of sun can never do,
Although its flashing fire is very strong.
And now no longer dallying with promises,
I will expound the ways of thunderbolts,
How they are made and what their force,
That they can blast a mighty tower apart,

257

Uproot a house and pick up beams and joists,
Tear up and overthrow the solid monuments of powerful men
Take life from human kind,
And strew in death the herds and flocks on every side.
The power in thunderbolts to do these things
And things like these, I'll show
We have to think that thunderbolts are borne from densest clouds,
Piled up on high;
For none was ever hurled from sky serene and clear,
Nor from a slight array of cloud.
Assuredly clear evidence
Shows us that this is so.
At times like these
Clouds form a dense array all through the air;
So one might think
That blackest shades of hell had left the underworld
And filled the mighty caverns of the sky.
So dreadful are the forms of murky fear that shadow us
When once this inky night of clouds has formed,
When once the storm begins to hurl its thunderbolts.
Quite often too a thick black cloud
Falls on the sea,
Just like a streaming flood of pitch—
Comes streaming down upon the waters of the deep.
Even afar this cloud seems packed with murk and gloom,
And seems to bring along a storm,
Teeming with thunderbolts and hurricanes,
Itself packed full with fire and wind;
So much that even men on shore
Will rush for shelter while their whole frame quakes.
Just so above our heads, we must suppose,
The storm hangs high;
Nor could the clouds shroud earth in such a thick and murky gloom

Unless they reared their palaces on high,
Cloud upon cloud,
To blot out every ray of sun.
Nor yet when came the rains
Could clouds so overwhelm the earth
To make the rivers flood and low plains swim
Unless the air were filled with cloud on cloud piled up on high.
But all this dense array of clouds
Is full of winds and fire; and thunder claps and lightning flash
Abound on every side.
Sometime ago I showed
That hollow clouds conceal atomic forms of heat in multitude;
Likewise in multitude receive them from the rays and heat of sun.
And when this self-same wind that drove them to one spot
Has squeezed out many atom shapes of heat,—
Itself has mingled with that heat,
Then the swift whirling eddy makes its way within,
And whirls around in close confines,
And in these blazing furnaces heats up the thunderbolt.
For two fold is the force that kindles this—
The friction of its own swift rush,
And contact with the fire.
Then when the power of wind has grown exceeding hot,
When fierce assault of fire has entered in,
The thunderbolt full grown, suddenly cleaves the cloud, comes hur-
                                                        tling out
And floods the whole of space with flashing light.
Then comes a grievous crash.
The temples of the sky seem suddenly
To burst apart and want to fall on us.
And then a tremble and a thrill runs through the earth,
And rumblings seem to rush through lofty sky.
Almost the whole storm cloud then trembles and quakes.

Mighty noises move abroad.
After the shock comes rain—abundant, heavy, dense,
So that the whole of sky seems turned to rain,
And its torrential fall seems to bring back the days of Noah.
So dreadful is the shower that issues forth from rending of the cloud,
When thunderbolts leap out with blazing blows.
Sometimes too,
The rushing force of wind strikes from outside
Upon the sturdy cloud, big with its ripened thunderbolt.
And when it cleaves the cloud there issues out straightway
That eddying rush of fire which we still call
As did our fathers long ago, a thunderbolt.
And this same thunderbolt pours out to other parts of earth and sky
Wherever force of wind has carried it.
Sometimes it happens too that wind
Though starting without fire,
Yet starts to blaze on its long course and random wandering.
For as it moves wind loses in its course
Some larger bits of matter; these cannot, like others
Make their way through air.
And smaller bits it gathers from the air and bears along
And these combining with the blast of wind produce the fire.
Just as often in its course a ball of lead grows hot,
By dropping atom forms of stiffening cold, taking up forms of fire.
It often happens too,
That of the very blow itself the force can stir up fire,
When wind itself, launched cold without its fire
Has struck its blow upon the cloud.
Because assuredly when wind has struck with violent blow
The particles of heat can stream together from the wind itself
And from the thing which then received the blow;
Just as when we strike a piece of stone with iron,
Fire issues forth;

Nor do the seeds of blazing heat rush slower to the blow,
Because the iron is cold.
So then a thing must blaze at blows of thunderbolts,
If it is fit and fitly placed to take the flame.
Nor should we rashly think that power of wind can be entirely cold
When launched with such amazing force on high.
If early in its course it's not aflame
It still arrives warmed up and mixed with heat.
The headlong speed and heavy blows of thunderbolts occur
And claps of thunder run their course with swift descent
Because the power of thunderbolts within the clouds
Sets self in motion of itself,
Collects itself within;
And then attempting to break forth
Acquires a mighty power to move.
Thus when the clouds no longer can contain
The great increasing powers of its assault,
The thunderbolt is squeezed outside the cloud,
And so flies on with wonderful velocity and power,
Like missiles from a mighty cannon hurled.
Think too that thunderbolts
Are formed of atom shapes most small and smooth;
So nothing easily could stand against and block
Substance like this.
It flits between and penetrates atomic pores of other things,
Is not delayed or clogged by many obstacles
And so sweeps on, in great power and velocity.
Then too, because by law of gravity all weights fall down,
If to their natural fall a blow is joined
Their speed is doubled and their downward smash is great indeed;
With greater power and speed they move,
To scatter with their blows whatever blocks their way.
They move majestic on their path.

Then too because the thunderbolt
Comes with a long and far assault
It ever gathers speed afresh, speed which increases as it moves,
Builds up its sturdy strength and makes more terrible its blows.
And so its very speed ensures
That all the atom structure of the thunderbolt
Is borne straight down, collected to one spot,
And all its several parts compelled to traverse the same course.
It could be too,
That, as it goes, the thunderbolt
Drags from the air itself some certain atom forms
Which by their blows inflame its swift velocity.
It comes to many things without destroying them,
It goes through many things and leaves them still unharmed,
Because its liquid fire can trickle through the pores.
And many things it pierces through
Since body of the thunderbolt itself falls on the very frame of things
                                                                outside,
Just where their fastenings bind and keep them one.
And bronze the thunderbolt can melt quite easily; gold it makes boil,
Because the structure of the thunderbolts is made exquisitely
Of tiny bodies, lightest atom forms.
These tiny shapes can easily
Worm their way through anything,
And having wormed their way
They suddenly break up the knots which held the thing and break its
                                                                bonds.

The house of sky with marvellous embroidery of twinkling stars
And all the earth around,
Is shaken in the autumn more by thunderbolts;
Or else when spring's gay time of flowers unfolds.
In time of winter's cold, fires fail;
In summer's heat the clouds come not,

Or if they do, come not so dense.
And so when heaven's season's poised between the two
Then all the various causes of the thunderbolt can coincide.
For then the narrow crossroads of the year
Can mix both heat and cold
And both of these the cloud must have to forge a thunderbolt,
That strife may be of thing with thing,
And aether in a furious storm may toss with fires and winds.
The coming-on of heat must be the end of stiffening cold.
That is the time of spring.
(And so opposing principles must clash, create a fight.)
And then again when last of summer's heat comes rolling in
Mingled with first attack of winter's cold,
(I mean, of course, the season that we call the fall)
Then too the piercing winter's cold in battle joins
With summer's heat.
And so it's right
To call the spring and fall the crossroads of the year
Nor is it wonderful at times like these
That thunderbolts come thick and fast;
A frightful tempest gathers in the sky,
Since furious battle rages either side,
Here joins in fight with flames
And there with winds and waters mixed.

The poet refutes superstitious notions about thunderbolts

THIS is the scientific way to know the power of thunderbolts;
The force by which they manage everything.
And not unlock the rolls of Tuscan prophesies
Or seek in vain to find some hint
Of what the hidden purpose of the gods—
Whence came the wingéd flash, or where it went,
Or how it made its way through walls;

Came out again the master of the house.
Or what harm heaven's thunderbolt can do to us.
If Jupiter and other heavenly deities
Can shake the gleaming temples in the sky with awe-inspiring crash,
And hurl the fire wherever each of them may will,
Why do they not ensure that those who do some awful deed
From which a decent man averts his face
Should feel the blow with breast transfixed
And reek with lightning's fire?
For this would be the sharpest kind of lesson to the human race.
Why is it that a man
Who knows that he is free from sin and innocent
Is suddenly entangled in the flames,
Caught in the whirlwind of celestial fire?
Why do they aim at desert spots and work in vain?
Perhaps at times like these,
The gods are training in the manual of arms
Or giving muscles exercise!
Or why do gods allow
That weapons of all powerful Jove be blunted in the earth?
Does Jove himself allow a thing like this,
Not keep the thunderbolt to use against his foes?
And why does Jupiter never hurl his thunderbolts to earth,
Pour out their sounding crash,
When sky is clear on every side?
Perhaps when clouds collect in sky
Jove then comes down to them
To hurl the weapons at his mark from shorter range!
With what idea in mind would Jove
Direct his thunder at the sea?
What accusation could he level at the waves,
The mass of moving waters and the swimming plains?
And if it is the will of Jove,

That men avoid the blows of thunderbolts
Why does he hesitate to let men see them hurled?
And if it is his wish
To catch us off our guard and smash us with the fire,
Why does he thunder from the self-same place
And put us on our guard?
Why does he gather in advance
Thick darkness, mighty cracks and rumbling roars?
And how could one believe
That Jove hurls many thunderbolts on many sides at once?
Or would you dare to hold that many thunderbolts have never hap-
                                                          pened
Simultaneously.
No. Many times this has come to be before and will again
When rains come tumbling down in many places at one time,
That many thunderbolts occurred
At one time, too.
And why does god in wrath
Smash up the sacred shrines of gods, their glorious resting place?
Why does he tear apart the shapely, well-wrought images of gods,
And spoil their loveliness with violent wounds?
Why does he aim at mountain tops so much,
That men should seem to see on mountain tops,
Most frequent traces of Jove's fire?

Meteorological phenomena: d) Watersprouts, Clouds, Rainbows

Now next in order you could learn quite easily
By this same method of research
How presters (watching their action the Greeks have given them this
                                                          name)
How presters hurled from far aloft
Have come into the sea.
Sometimes it comes about

That something like a column lowered from the sky
Descends into the sea.
The surges boil around, stirred by the violent, breathing blasts,
And any ship that's in the turmoil caught
Is tossed about and comes to danger's uttermost.
Now this occurs when winds once set to move,
Cannot break the cloud from which they try to burst,
But down they push the massive clouds,
So that they seem a column, lowered from the sky to sea;
As though a fist and arms above
Pushed down the column bit by bit,
Extended it across the waves.
And when its torn the cloud apart,
The violent wind bursts out and hits the sea,
Creates a marvellous tumult in the waves;
Down comes the whirling eddy and brings down
The pliant cloud
And when it brings the pregnant cloud to ocean's level waves
The eddy suddenly comes hurtling down
Plunges itself completely into Ocean's deep
And with a mighty roar stirs up the sea
And makes it seethe.
Then too,
A whirling eddy of the winds can wrap itself in clouds
And gather seeds of cloud from air,
And imitate the prester let down from sky.
Now when this eddy has let itself descend to earth and broken up,
It vomits out a furious force of whirlwind and of storm.
(A thing like this, of course, is rarely seen;)
And if one watches from the land, mountains obscure the view,
It's seen more frequently
On open waters of the sea or vast expanse of sky,
And now, to touch another theme, clouds collect

266

When many bodies flying through the upper reaches of the air
Have come together suddenly—
Bodies of rougher texture so that they cohere
Though only slightly intertwined.
These bodies first of all cause little clouds to form.
These then in turn assemble, congregate,
And grasp each other with a mutual grip,
And, as they join, they grow and by the winds are borne along,
Until at last a furious storm appears.
And mountain tops, the more they tower to the sky
The more their peaks smoke constantly with murky darkness of a
tawny cloud,
Because when first the cloud mass forms, while still the clouds are
rarer that the eye can see
The winds bear them along, assemble them on mountain tops.
And there, dense now, assembled in a greater throng
At last they can be seen,
And seem to mount the open sky from mighty mountain top.
The fact itself the vision of our sense proclaims
That when we climb the mountainside
Windy regions stretch above.
Then too that nature raises up such bodies from the sea,
And many of them everywhere
Is proved by clothes hung by the shore
That take and hold the clinging dew.
And so it's clear
That many bodies rise to swell the cloud from salty surges of the sea.
(The moisture of the sea and clouds is closely kin.)
Then too, from every stream and from the earth itself
We often see vapours and clouds arise
And these ascend like breath;
Then borne aloft, they cover sky with curtain of the inky cloud
And bit by bit they meet and form the clouds aloft.

And starry aether's heat above presses them down
Compresses them and makes them weave a web of cloud beneath the
blue.

From outside too,
Those bodies come which go to make the clouds and whirling storms.
For I have often shown that atom forms
Are countless in their multitude
And infinite the vast extent of sky.
And I have shown how fast the atoms fly,
How instantaneously they flash across a space,
Beyond the power of men to tell.
So then it's not so wonderful if in the shortest space of time
Storm clouds and darkness cover up the sea and land
And brood above;
Since from all around
Through all the pores of aether and the breathing spaces of the mighty
world
The atom forms can enter or depart.
Come now I will unfold
How rainy moisture gathers in the lofty clouds
And how the shower shoots down and falls upon the earth.
First then I'll prove
That many seeds of moisture rise from everything;
When clouds rise up, these seeds rise too;
That both thus grow alike—
The clouds and all the moisture that's contained in clouds;
Just as the human body grows along with human blood,
And likewise sweat and all the moisture that's within our limbs.
Then too,
The clouds take in abundant moisture from the sea
When headlong winds are driving them across the deep;
Just as a fleece of wool will soak up dew.
In this way too,

Water out of countless streams is raised on high.
And so,
When many seeds of water have assembled in a thousand ways,
On every side have found increase,
The dense packed clouds then long to lose their moisture for a two-
fold cause.
The power of wind drives it along.
The very multitude of clouds collected in a great array
And pushing from above,
Makes rains stream out in copious shower.
Then too,
When clouds are scattered by the winds or broken up,
Smitten above by rays of sun,
They send their moisture out and drip
As lighted tapers held above a scorching fire
Drip fast.
And so a violent storm of rain occurs
When clouds are roughly squeezed by either force—
Their piling up, or by the force of wind.
The rains stay long
When seeds of water congregate in multitude
And cloud is piled on cloud;
And dripping mists above are borne from everyside;
When all earth steams,
And gives back moisture in the form of breath.
At times like these,
When sun reveals its rays amid the murky storm,
When spray from clouds confronts the sun,
A rainbow's colours then are seen among black clouds.
Now all the other things that come to be in sky,
And all the things that grow in sky and gather in the clouds—
Snow and winds and hail and chilly frosts,
The mighty power of ice, strong to rein in swift streams,

To learn the laws of all is not so hard,
To understand how they have come to be,
And how they're made,
When once you've learned the power to atom stuff assigned.

Unusual terrestrial phenomena: Earthquakes

OF earthquakes now come learn the laws.
Imagine first that just as all above the earth is filled with windy caves
Just so it is below;
That mother earth bears in her mighty womb,
A multitude of lakes and pools and cliffs and towering rocks;
That many streams are hidden underneath her spine
To roll in torrent force their waves with rolling stones,
(For common sense demands we think,
That earth is everywhere alike.)
Since these beneath the earth are placed and joined,
The upper part of earth will quake
When, underneath, time makes great caverns tumble in—
The fall of mighty masses down below
Makes upper levels shake.
Sometimes indeed,
Whole mountains fall and at the great and sudden shock,
Tremors spread far and wide.
No wonder;
For you've often seen how all a house,
If built beside the road,
Trembles and shakes,
Though passing waggon be but light.
And waggons leap when stones upon the road,
Jolt the iron circles of the wheels on either side.
It happens too that when a mighty mass of soil
Is loosed by time from earth

And, rolling down, comes into great wide watery pools,
That earth then sways and totters at the shock
Of water's surging waves.
Just as a vase at times cannot stand still
Unless the liquid it contains stands too,
No longer surges here and there in choppy waves.
Then too,
When the wind is gathered through the caverns of the earth
Blows strong from some one point,
And strives and pushes on the lofty caves with mighty strength
The earth inclines towards the point
Where headlong force of wind is pushing it.
And then the houses that are built upon the surface of the earth
The loftier they are, the more they tower towards the sky
The more they bend and hang,
Totter towards the quarter of the world where wind is pushing them.
And all their beams protrude and seem prepared to fall.
And yet men hesitate to think
That earth will one day fall in ruin,
Even though they see so great a fraction of the earth
Totter towards its fall.
But were it not that winds must pause and catch their breath,
No force could hold things in,
Nor keep them back from ruin as they fell.
But as it is,
Because in turn winds storm and pause in turn to breathe
Because like hosts in combat joined,
They now reform their ranks and charge,
And now again retreat, fall back,
Destruction is more often threatened by the earth
Than made.
For often earth leans over and then sways back again,

And, after falling forward, brings its weight
Back to its proper place
And so it comes about that all a building quakes,
The top part most of all, the middle less; the bottom hardly moves.
Now this cause, too, might cause a dreadful quake,
When winds and powerful streams of air have met,
Gathered either from within, or sometimes from without the earth,
Have hurled their might within the caverns of the earth,
And rage amid the caves, and sweep about in whirls.
And then the awful energy of wind is driven forth, bursts out,
And cleaves the earth right to its very depths, making an awful cleft.
For so it happened once at Sidon—a distant Phrygian town,
And Sparta's neighbour, Aegium—
These towns were overthrown by just such whirl of wind as I've
                                                              described,
And the ensuing quake of earth.
And many other great walled towns
Have fallen through great movements of the land,
And many hurtled down to Ocean's deeps, cities and peoples both.
And though the wind does not burst forth
Yet still its wild assault and headlong energy
Are spread abroad,
Like tremors through the many passages beneath the earth
And there induce a trembling
Just as a chill, assailing human limbs,
Shakes them against our will
And makes the human quake and shake.
And so through mighty towns,
Men also quake with two-fold fear.
They fear the falling buildings up above,
They fear the hollow places underneath—
Lest earthquakes break them open all at once,

Lest earth should open up a gaping cleft
And will to fill it up with jumbled ruins.
No matter all their firm beliefs
That earth will evermore endure
Because entrusted to the guiding hand of god
Yet nonetheless the sudden imminence of threats
On this side or on that
Digs in the sharpened goad of fear—
Lest earth be snatched from underneath their feet
And suddenly;
Lest earth be hurled down in the deep abyss
And all the universe should sway and perish utterly,
Become a total wreck.

The sea is constant in size

AND first of all some men feel awe
That bounteous nature in her care for men
Does not make seas increase
Though rains torrential keep pouring in
And all the streams from every side of earth.
Add too the wandering showers of flying storms,
Which drench and sprinkle all the seas and lands.
Add too the springs from Ocean's depths.
And yet compared with vastness of the sea
All these are hardly equal to a single drop.
And so it is no miracle
That mighty sea increases not.
Then too the sun draws off a part—great part
Of Ocean's moisture with his heat.
We see him with his blazing rays
Dry clothes though sopping wet.
And yet we see
Wide oceans very many spread before our eyes.

And though the sun draws very little water from a given space,
Yet from the waves of Ocean's wide expanse,
He draws up water copiously;
And winds, sweeping the level sea pick up much wet.
Often we see the roads grow dry in just one night,
The soft mud harden into cakes.
Then too I've shown
That clouds can lift and raise much moisture from the vast expanse
of sea,

Again in turn distribute it through all the circle of the lands,
When on the earth the torrent falls,
And winds drive clouds.
Now last of all
Since matter out of which the earth is made
Is porous,
And with this porous earth the sea is joined
Encircling every coast,
It needs must be
That moisture filter back to land from Ocean's salty deeps
Just as the moisture passes from the lands and joins the sea.
The brine is filtered off, the moisture trickles back
Assembles at the source of every stream
Thence flows through earth in torrent fresh
Wherever once a way is cut
To let the waters run in liquid march.

Volcanic eruptions

AND now I'll tell
Why through the jaws of Aetna flames at times breathe forth
In dreadful hurricane of fire.
The fiery tempest rose with havoc terrible
And like a tyrant ranged the fields of Sicily
And turned the face of neighbouring nations to itself,

As people saw the temples of the sky sparkle and smoke,
While fear filled human hearts to contemplate
The basic change in things that nature wrought.
And now in this your study must go far and deep,
And wide the view you take on every side,
Remembering that the total of the universe is infinite,
You must perceive
How tiny, insignificant is just one heaven.
It's like comparing just one man to all the earth.
Now keep this fact before you, ponder it,
Look at it clearly and as clearly see;
No longer will you gape in wonder at so many things.
Would any man alive be lost in wonder if he saw
A man feel in his limbs,
A fever burning with a fiery heat,
Or any other pain, disease?
Sometimes a foot will swell;
Often a piercing pang will strike the teeth;
Or soreness seizes on the very eyes.
A sacred fire bursts forth
And creeps through human frame,
And burns the part which it has seized
Creeps through the limbs,
Because assuredly,
Atoms exist of many things.
This earth of ours, this sky,
Has sickness and malady enough
Whence measureless disease might spread abroad.
Just so then we suppose
That from the infinite reservoir of things
All things are given all the earth and sky,
Enough that on a sudden earth herself could quake and move,
A headlong whirlwind race o'er seas and lands,

And Ætna's fires well up and all the sky take fire.
Now all this comes to pass and more;
The heavenly temples blaze;
In close packed concourse rains and storms will congregate
To bring torrential rain,
When it so happens that the atom forms of water so arrange them-
selves.

But one will say
'This fiery storm and blaze is very big.'
And so it is.
Just as a river will seem big,
To one who has not seen a larger one before;
Just as a man, a tree seem big,
And anything that goes beyond a man's experience,
These he thinks huge.
Yet all of them with earth and sky and ocean too
Are nothing by comparison
With all the infinite total of the universe.
And now I'll tell
How flame is suddenly stirred up, breathes out
From Aetna's mighty furnaces.
First point;—
The mountain's hollow underneath
And everywhere is propped on vaults of flint.
Next point:—
In all the caves is wind and air.
(For air you know is wind when set in motion, stirred, aroused.)
Now when this wind is hot and in its furious course
Has heated all the rocks and earth wherever it has touched,
And from these rocks and earth has struck
Terrific fire with leaping flames,
It then leaps up and drives itself outside
Straight through the mountain jaws.

And then its heat spreads far and wide,
The ash is scattered far,
While murky smoke and blackness roll along
And rocks of monstrous weight come shooting out.
All this you must not doubt is caused by stormy force of air.
Then too the sea forces its breaking waves
Against the roots and base of that same mount,
Sucks back its surf again.
Now from this sea hollow caves extend
Right to the lofty jaws and summit of the hill.
We must confess that by this path wind and the waves pass through,
Compel the various substances—water and sand and stones
To penetrate deep in from open sea
Then the volcano breathes them out,
And by the energy of rushing wind breathes flame,
And casts out rocks and raises clouds of dust.
(The text here is corrupt and it is impossible to know with certainty
                                        just what Lucretius meant.)
For on the highest peaks are bowls (Craters some may say.
This is the natives' name for them; we call them jaws or mouths.)

The Nile

MANY strange things occur for which it's not enough to give one cause.
Several we cite but one of these must be the actual cause.
If you should see a man lie dead before your eyes,
You'd be doing right to cite all possible causes for his death
That you might hit the one.
You could not prove
That he had died by violence or from cold,
By poison or disease,
We know that one of these has caused his death.
Of several natural wonders could the same be said.
The river Nile that crosses Egypt's whole extent

277

Rises as summer comes, overflows the plains
And is the only river in the world that does the like.
Often when summer's at its height it floods Egyptian plains,
Either because in summer
North winds blow against the mouths of river Nile—
The Etesian winds blow at that time of year—;
These press against the stream and check its course;
Driving the waters back they fill the channel of the stream
And make the waters pause.
Without a doubt these winds
Which start beneath the chill star of the northern pole
Drive hard against the stream.
The Nile itself comes from the sultry southern parts
Far inland from the regions of mid-day
Where live the copper, sunburned, dark-complexioned men.
It may be too
That heaps of sand pile up against the river mouths
And check the current of the stream,
When sea stirred up by heavy winds drives sand within.
And so it comes about
That exit for the water is less free
The waves flow down less easily.
Perhaps more rains occur in summer at the sources of the Nile
When northern, Etesian winds
Collect all clouds in regions whence the river comes.
And when these clouds are driven to the regions of mid-day,
Then they
Are gathered there, confined in little space,
Pushed to the mountain tops and there compressed.
Or then perhaps the Nile
Is fed and swollen deep within the mountains of the Ethiopians
Where sun, traversing everything with melting rays
Makes the white snows run down into the plains.

Places and lakes that are fatal to birds

COME now I will unfold and tell
The nature of the places called Avernian.
(Avernus, Greek Aornos, means the birdless place.)
In that they're called Avernian, the name is given from the fact
These places bring a fatal malady to every kind of bird.
For when birds fly over them
Forgetful of the oarage of their wings
They slack their sails and fall—
With drooping necks they fall to earth,
(If earth is there below;
Or into water if by chance the lake Avernus lies beneath.
That place is near to Cumae, where the mountains smoke,
Choked with sharp sulphur, bounteous with hot and steaming
                                                    springs,)
Within the walls of Athens too,
High on the very summit of the citadel,
Hard by Athena's fane—Athena, guardian of the city folk below;
Here the cawing crows
Never steer their bodies on the wing,
Though altars smoke with sumptuous offerings.
It is not as the Grecian poets sang
Athena's fiery wrath they shun
Because the crows had spied on her;
Rather the nature of the place keeps crows away.
In Syria, too, men say there is a place
Where if a four-legged beast just touches it,
The poison of the place will knock him down,
And heavily he'd fall
Like victims slaughtered suddenly to guardian spirits of the dead.
Yet all these come about by natural law.
The cause of the event can easily be seen.

So that you do not think it possible
That in the place there is a gate of Hell
And so believe that guardian spirits of the dead
Lead souls below and bring them to the shores of Acheron.
Just as some men believe that stags with winged feet
Can sniff and summon crawling serpents from their lairs.
Now learn from me how far from truth is such a tale.
For now I try to speak about the fact itself.
So first I say as I have often said before
That on the earth are shapes of things of every kind—
Many which serve for food preserving life,
Many which bring disease and hasten death.
Then too, I've shown
That for the life of different creatures different things will serve
(The nature of these different creatures is unlike,
Their texture is unlike,
Unlike the atom forms from which they're made.)
And many hurtful things pass through the ears
And many dangerous things, things rough to touch
Pass through the nose;
And some there are which we should shun to touch,
Yes even see,
And some are bitter to the taste.
Then we may see
How many things induce in man
Sensations quite unpleasant, noisome, even nauseous.
Some trees have shade so poisonous
That if one lies beneath and stretches on the grass
They cause a racking pain throughout the head.
And on the lofty hills of Helicon there is a tree
Which kills a man with poisonous odour of its flower.
Now all these things grow from the earth like this

Assuredly because the earth contains within itself
The many atom forms of many things,
Mingled in many ways.
And earth then separates them and sends them out.
If you blow out a lamp at night
Its acrid smell assails the nose and puts to sleep
Even an epileptic man—a man who falls, foams at the mouth.
A woman can be put to sleep by heavy scent of oil,
Emitted by the beaver;
The gay embroidery slips from her dainty hands
If she has sniffed the smell while in her monthly period.
And many other scents can leave the limbs relaxed throughout the
frame
And make the human life to quail throughout its bodily abode.
After a heavy meal if you should dally in the tub
And wash yourself* and linger in the steaming heat
How often you collapse and faint.
How easily the noxious fume of charcoal
Finds its way into the brain
Unless before we smell the fumes we've taken water in.
But if a raging fever has taken hold of one
And tamed one's limbs,
Then the smell of wine
Falls like the blow of pole axe on a slaughtered beast.
You see that sulphur formed in earth herself
And asphalt
Harden into crusts with stench most horrible,
When men are following up the veins of silver and of gold,
Probing the hidden parts of earth with picks;
Scaptensula (in Thrace) breathes out most awful odors then.
And mines of gold, what poisons they emit!
What faces, what complexions they produce in men.

* Translating *Lueris* Diels.

You must have seen and heard how miners die so young,
And how the vital forces fail in men
Whom stern compulsion imprisons in a job like that.
These odours then the earth sends steaming forth
Breathes them into open air and open stretches of the sky.
So then, to sum the matter up
Those spots we call Avernian must send up fumes that prove
Deadly to birds;
These fumes rise up from earth to sky
And in these parts they poison heaven's expanse.
So when the bird is borne there on its wings
There it is checked, seized by the fatal effluence
Just where the poison places it;
And when the bird has fallen down,
The same miasma takes the rest of life from all its limbs.
First it brings on a kind of dizziness;
And afterwards
When they've fallen in the poison's very fount and source
There life they vomit out,
Because the poison lies so thick around.
It may be too at times Avernus' poisoned power
Dispels the air that lies between the birds and earth
And leaves a void between.
And when the flying birds have crossed this void
Their wings will suddenly flutter, useless and limp.
And all the effort of the wings on either side is vain.
Then when they cannot rest or lean upon their wings
Nature compels them, wings and all, to sink to earth
By their own weight;
And then they lie in death in what is almost empty void,
And give their life abroad through all the body's pores.
(Some lines are lost at this point.)

Strange fountains

THE water in deep wells grows cold in summer
Because the earth becomes more porous with the heat.
And if perchance th' water itself has any atom forms of heat
It lets them go, escape into the air.
The more the earth grows old, worn out with heat,
The colder grows the moisture hidden in the earth.
And, when the whole of earth is crushed by cold
The earth contracts, congeals,
And as it shrinks it squeezes down into the wells
The heat it bears itself.
Men say that hard by Ammon's shrine in Libya
A fountain rises, in the daytime cold and warm at night.
Men marvel at this wonder far too much.
And some men think that water in the spring is made to boil
By fierce hot rays of sun, when sun has passed beneath the earth.
When night has covered earth with darkness terrible.
Now this is very far from valid inference.
If the sun
Touching from above the naked body of the earth
Could not make the water hot,
How could it underneath the earth
Then when the body it must penetrate
Is very dense,
Make water boil and glut it with a wealth of heat,
When with its blazing rays the sun can scarcely penetrate
A house's walls?
What is the truth?
It's certain that around the spring
The earth is rarer than the norm;
And near the water there are many atom forms of fire,
And when night overwhelms the earth with dewy waves
Straightway deep down the earth grows cold, contracts;

And just as when a sponge is squeezed by hand
The earth expels the atom forms of fire
And puts them in the spring.
And so the water and the spring feel warm to touch.
Then when the rising sun has loosened up the soil
And made it porous as the steaming heat disturbs the earth,
The atom forms of fire take up their old abode again
And all the heat that once the water had
Returns into the earth.
And so on this account,
The spring grows cold under the light of day.
The water too is buffeted by rays of sun
And as the daylight grows, its texture grows more thin
Through quivering surge of heat
And so it loses all the atom forms of fire.
Just as often water will lose the frost it has—
The ice will melt and all its fastenings relax.
There is a cold spring too;
And, if you hold some tinder over it,
It straightway catches fire, gives out a flame.
A torch, too, catches fire and gleams
A blazing beacon on the surface of the spring,
Wherever breath of breezes pushes it.
Because assuredly
There lurk in waters of the spring
A multitude of atom forms of heat;
And from the earth itself at bottom of the spring,
These atom forms of heat rise up through all the waters of the spring,
Rise up like breath and come into the air.
Yet there are not enough of them to make the fountain hot.
And, scattered as they are, their energy
Makes them burst out from water one by one,
And meet above.

At Aradus there is a spring within the sea.
The water that this spring pours forth is fresh,
It parts the salty water all around.
And elsewhere too the level sea gives help to thirsty mariners,
By pouring out fresh water mid the salty waves.
So then in just this way
These seeds of heat can burst a way,
Emerge through that same spring and bubble out.
When they collect around the tinder, cling to the torch,
They blaze out all at once,
Because the tinder and the torch have many seeds of fire themselves.
See also how you place a taper near a lamp at night
That's just gone out.
Without a contact with the wick the taper blazes; torches too.
And many other things are made to blaze by heat alone
By distant contact long before the fire can steep them close at hand.
And this we must suppose can happen in that fountain too.

Magnets

Now for the rest I will begin to tell
By which of Nature's laws it comes about
That iron is drawn along by th' attraction of that stone
Which from its native place the Greeks have called the magnet
                                                            stone.
(It is found in country of the Magnetes.)
Men wonder at this stone.
The stone can make a chain of rings hang to itself.
Five or six you often see hang in a chain and sway in every breeze,
Each clinging to the next,
As each one feels compulsive power, attraction of the magnet stone.
For so its power prevails by seeping through.
In each investigation of this kind we must establish much
Before we give a rational account of what we're out to find.

The thing itself we must approach by long and winding path.
And so the more I ask attentive mind and ears.
First then from everything we see
Atomic forms must stream, shoot out, be spread abroad,
To strike our eyes, awake our sense.
Odors stream out from other things unceasingly—
Just as the cold from streams; heat from the sun;
Spray from the waves of sea—
The spray which eats the sea wall by the ocean's shore.
And many different kinds of sound ooze through the air unceasingly.
Often will moist and salty taste assail the mouth,
Or when we watch a dose of wormwood being mixed
Its bitter taste assails.
And so from everything must bodies flow, scatter on every side.
Nor is delay or respite granted to the stream,
Since sense is active constantly;
We never cease to see and smell and hear.
Come now I'll tell again of what rare stuff all things are made.
This I have clearly shown as I began this work.
And though for many reasons we must know these things,
For this it is most necessary—
That we should know that nothing ever can be perceived
Save these two principles—atoms and void.
In rocks and caves the waters trickle through
And all things seem to weep with copious drops.
From all our body sweat oozes out;
And hair and whiskers grow on human face and all our limbs;
Food can creep through veins of every living thing
To bring increase and nourishment even to members most remote,
Even to tiny nails.
We feel that cold and heat can pass through bronze;
We feel it pass through silver and through gold,
When brimming cups we hold in both our hands.

Voices can go through walls of stone;
Odors and cold and fire's tremendous heat.
(Why this can even penetrate the strength of iron.)
And where the breastplate of the sky enfolds the world around
Blind bodies from outside make their way in,
Afflict the race of men and beasts with countless maladies—
The baleful energy of sickness as the atoms find their way within.*
Storms too arising in the sky and on the earth,
Are naturally absorbed and disappear on earth and sky.
For nothing lies between that is not made of porous stuff.
There is this further fact,
That not all atom particles thrown off from different things
Have the same power to touch our sense,
Nor equally are suited for all things
The sun will bake the ground and make it hard,
While ice it thaws;
And makes the snow piled high on mighty hills
Soon melt away.
And wax when placed to catch the heat of sun will melt.
Fire too will make bronze liquid, break up gold.
But skin and flesh are shrivelled, drawn together by the fire.
Water will temper iron
When iron is drawn red hot from smithy fire;
But skin and flesh when hardened by the heat
It softens up.
The olive growing wild will bring delight to bearded goats
As much as though it breathed ambrosia
As much as though it were in nectar steeped;
But for a man no plant that grows
Is such a bitter morsel to the taste.*
Marjoram pigs avoid and every kind of ointment shun

* Translating Diel's emendation.
* Translating *esca*.

287

These things are poison to the bristling pigs,
And yet to us they seem to give new life.
And though to us the mud is vilest filth,
It seems most pleasant to a pig
Who'll wallow in the mud and roll from head to foot
And never have enough.
Now this too must be said,
Before I speak about the magnet stone itself.
Since many pores are spread through different things
Differ they must.
For each must have its own arrangement of material stuff
With passages between.
For different organs of the sense
Are present in the various living things
By which they grasp the objects peculiarly their own.
By one of these a sound can penetrate our consciousness,
And by another tastes, by yet another smell.
One thing can make its way through rocks,
Another thing through wood, through gold a third;
While yet another one can go abroad from silver or from glass.
Through one a vision makes its way,
And through another heat.
And even when the stuff's the same, the passages the same
One thing will make its way more quickly than another one.
The nature of the pores so infinitely various
Compels these differences as we have shown before.
Now when all this has been established and laid down,
And set in due array before our eyes,
The rest we'll find quite easy to explain
With all its causes manifest,
Why iron for all its strength
Can be seduced, enticed;
First from this stone must flow

A multitude of atom forms;
Perhaps a surge which with its blows
Parts all the air that lies between the iron and magnet stone.
And when this space between is emptied out,
Becomes a void,
Straightway the atom particles of iron rush in
In thronging numbers and together joined.
And then the ring comes too
And with its total bulk moves in.
(For nothing as you know is quite so closely joined,
In nothing do the atom forms more closely cling
Than chilling roughness and the sturdy strength of iron)
And so it's not remarkable
Because the ring is pulled on by its elements
(If many particles arising from the iron,
Springing together in their multitude
Cannot as individuals pass into the void,)
That ring should follow too.*
And so the ring will follow on,
Until it comes to magnet stone itself,
And clings to it because of hidden dark attractive power,
And this occurs on every side.
Wherever space becomes a void,
Whether above or on the side
The particles around are straightway drawn into the void.
You see; the atoms in the rear
Are set in motion by atomic blows
Nor can they of themselves rise upwards into air.
A further factor helps.
This also helps the ring to move—
The fact that when the air before the ring
Becomes more rare, the place itself more void

* (The text here is corrupt. I think this is what it means. Translating *ducitur*, Lachmann.)

Then all the air behind
Propels and pushes it along.
The air which lies around is always striking things.
But at a time like this it moves the object on,
Because there is this empty space ahead which gathers in the ring.
This air of which I speak
Subtly wins its way to countless pores of iron
Into its smallest parts, pushes it on,
As ships are driven by their sails and wind.
For everything has air within its frame,
For everything is rarified in some degree,
And this same air surrounds all things, touches all things.
Now then this air that's hidden deep within the iron,
By constant restless motion ever tossed,
Buffets the ring without a doubt and stirs it from within.
And so the ring is borne along,
Strives hard to reach the empty spot
To which it, once has swooped.
It sometimes happens too that iron retreats
Before the onslaught of this stone,
And now advances, now retires.
I, myself, have seen the iron rings of Samothrace leap up;
I've seen iron filings in a frenzied dance
Whirling like maddened Maenads in a bowl,
When magnet stone was placed beneath
So passionately the iron desires, it seems,
To shun this stone.
When brass is placed between the turmoil is immense;
No doubt because the atoms emanating from the brass
First seize and occupy the pores within the iron;
And afterwards there comes an emanation from the stone
And finds the passages within the stone are all filled up,
Nor can it find a path to stream through as before.

And so it has to dash upon the iron,
And batter texture of the iron with dashing wave.
And so the magnet spits back from itself
The little chips of iron.
And through the bronze its power can penetrate
To set the iron in motion once again.
(But if the brass had not been there,
The magnet would absorb the filings back into itself.)
Now do not think this wonderful
That influences from this stone should not be strong enough
To drive all other things along as easily as these.
Sometimes they stand, resist,
Relying on the power of their own weight—
An instance, gold.
Sometimes the stuff of them is very rare,
And when the influence from the magnet stone
Passes right on through, untouched.
Such things cannot be driven anywhere;
And in this group is wood.
Iron lies between the two;
And when it takes within itself some atom forms of brass
Then the Magnesian stone can carry it along its torrent stream.
And yet this property of the magnet stone
Is not unknown in other things.
I have a scanty store of things like this to tell about:—
Things fitted for each other and for nothing else besides.
Stones cling with only mortar in between.
And wood is joined with nothing else than glue
That's made from carcass of the bull.
A board will quicker split and break
Than glued joints loose their hold.
The vine-born juice of grape will dare to mix,
Mingle with water in a running stream;

Yet pitch that's heavy, olive oil that's light refuse.
The shellfish's purple tint will mingle with wool alone
So closely that you cannot separate the two,
Not even though you try with all your might
To bring the whiteness back with help of Neptune's waves.
Not even though the multitudinous seas
Should strive to wash it out again with all its waves.
There's one thing only known to bind
Gold against gold.
And only tin can solder brass to brass.
We might find other cases too. What need?
Why should you tread a long and winding path of argument?
Why should I spend my time and pains on this?
Rather with just a word or two
I'll briefly comprehend them all.
Those things are joined the best
Whose structures are most opposite—
Solid to hollow, to concave convex.
And some things seem to cling, held together as if by hooks and eyes.
This seems to be the case with magnet and with iron.

And now the reasons for disease

AND now the reason for disease
And whence a plague can suddenly arise
To bring a deadly malady to men and herds
This I will tell.
First I have shown that many atom forms exist which help our life;
It must be too that many flit around to cause
Disease and death.
When these by chance arise, disturb the sky,
The atmosphere brings death.
That onslaught of disease and pestilence
Comes from outside to smite the world

Through sky above as do the clouds and mist,
Or else it gathers of itself and rises from the earth
When earth itself is moist,
When putrefaction grips the earth because of heavy rains.
You know how travellers when far from home and fatherland
Are bothered by the change in water that they drink,
By novelty of climate much distressed.
How different the climate that the Britons know
And that in Egypt where the axis of the world inclines.
How different Pontus and Cadiz,
And so on till we come to darker race of men with sunburnt hue.
As these four climates at the four winds of the earth,
Differ so much,
So the colour and the face of men
Must differ too;
So must diseases to attack the human race kind after kind.
The elephant disease occurs by streams of Nile*
In Attica men's feet are agonized by gout,
In Argolis the eyes feel pain.
And so each place harms different parts and limbs—
The varying air's the cause.
And so when any blast of wind harmful to us begins to move
And when this hostile breath begins to creep
In form of clouds or mists;
As bit by bit it makes its way to poison everything;
Then when at last it occupies our sky
This it corrupts and makes our sky above
Just like itself harmful to us.
And so this new disease and pestilence
Broods on the water, settles on the crops,
The food which beasts and men consume;
Or else remains poised in the air itself;

* *I.e.* Elephantiasis.

And when we breathe this tainted air
We breathe into our bodies foul disease.
Just so the pestilence will often fall
On cattle too and sluggish bleating sheep.
It's all the same
Whether we change the mantle of the sky
And visit those unfriendly spots;
Or whether nature should herself assail
With sky corrupt or new conditions to break down our health.

The great plague at Athens

A PLAGUE like this and gusty waves of death,
In Athens long ago filled fields with dead
And left its roadways desolate
And drained the town of citizens.
Born deep in Egypt,
Over swimming fields and wide extent of sky
It made its way and brooded at the last
Over all the folk of Cecrops' famous town.
In serried ranks they felt the sting of fell disease and death.
At first they felt the head with fever burn
And both eyes flare with inflammation red.
The blackened throat within was choked with blood,
While ulcers blocked the path of voice and utterance.
The tongue, the vocal spokesman of the brain,
Would ooze with blood,
Weakened with evils, slow in movement, rough to touch.
When through the throat the onset of disease
Had filled the breast and touched the very heart,
Then all the warden fortress of their life was broken down.
The breath poured noisome odours from their mouth,
Smells like the stench of rotten flesh, when thrown outdoors.
And straightway all the strength of mind and all the body's energy

Grew faint and dim,
As if the victim, even now, were at the gate of death.
And with their aching torments ever came
Anguish unutterable, mingled sobs and groans.
Continuous vomiting by night and day doubled them up,
Caused spasms in their weary limbs,
And broke their tired bodies down and wore them out.
In no case could you feel the surface and the topmost skin
Burn with excessive heat.
Rather the skin felt lukewarm to the touch.
And yet the whole was red with ulcer's flame,
As is the case when sacred fire burns through the limbs.
Within, meantime, the man was burning up right to the marrow
bones.

A fiery furnace blazed beneath his ribs.
No coverlet, though light and thin, would help at all,
Only a cooling breeze.
And some would hurl their sick and burning limbs
In waters cold, immerse their bodies bare in cooling waves.
Many leaped headlong into cold deep wells,
Striving with open mouths to quaff a cooling draught.
A thirst unquenchable, parching their scorching frames,
Made endless water seem like tiny drops.
Respite was none for evil; there they lay, done up.
In silent panic medicine muttered low.
When sufferers rolled their weary fevered eyes
Heralds of death.
And many other signs of death were there to note—
The troubled mind, in anguish plunged and fear,
The furrowed brow, the fierce and frenzied face,
The ringing ears, plagued and possessed with noise,
The quick tense breathing or great sudden pants,
The shining sweat that gleamed on neck and throat,

The thin rare phlegm, with yellow flecked and salt,
That coughing scarce could bring up through the throat.
Then in the hands the sinews would contract.
All limbs would tremble, and the cold
Inched slowly up the body from the feet.
To the last moment nostrils were compressed,
The tip of nose was sharpened like a quill.
Then eyes were hollowed, temples, too,
Skin hard and cold, a drooping grin on mouth,
Brow drawn and swollen.
A little later and the limbs were stiff in death.
And on the eighth bright day of shining sun,
Perhaps the ninth, they yielded up their life.
And if a man escaped the doom of death,
Yet afterwards a slow decay awaited him,
Noisome with ulcers and the bowels' black flux.
In many a case, while head would ache,
Foul blood flowed from his nose.
In this way ebbed away his whole reserve of body's strength.
If he survived this horrid flow of tainted blood,
Still the disease invaded nerves and limbs and even genitals.
In many a case, fearing the gates of death,
They suffered self-castration with a knife.
Some lingered on, deprived of hands and feet,
And some of eyes,
So firmly had a morbid fear of death seized hold of them.
For some all memory of things slipped right away—
They knew not who they were or where.
And though the corpses lay in serried ranks piled up,
The dogs and birds avoided them,
So strong the stench they made.
For, if they tasted, straightway dropped,
Struck by swift death.

In those days hardly any birds appeared at all,
No gloomy creatures issued from the woods.
They mostly fell, and drooped and died.
The loyal strength of dogs, though fighting hard,
Laid down its life, their corpses strewn through every street.
The dire power of plague would wrest
All power from all their limbs.
Meanwhile the sad untended funerals
Were rushed in rivalry, like contests at the games.
Nor could a single cure suggest itself,
To heal all men alike.
What aided one and gave him strength
To draw life giving air and gaze upon the temples of the sky,
To others brought destruction, death.
In all the havoc, this was most pitiable;
When a man saw himself entangled in disease,
As though condemned straightway to death, his courage fled.
He'd lay with grieving heart and look for death
And pour his spirit out.
The dark contagion of the greedy plague
Passed on from man to man,
Like havoc through a flock of wooly sheep or hornéd kine.
And so the plague heaped pyre on funeral pyre.
Too covetous of life and dreading death
Some paid for cowardice by coming to an end
Hard and disgraceful
Deserted, shameful, and bereft of help.
And those who stayed to help their kin
Died too—
Worn down by labour and by contact with disease—
The work that noble shame prompted to undertake—
The coaxing voice of misery mixed with complaints.

And so the noblest souls also met death.
And one by one they died,
As emulously they strove to lay at rest
The crowding dead.
And almost dead from mourning they'd come home again
And most of them were prostrate in their beds from grief.
In those awful times was no man found
Untouched by dreadful plague and death,
No one who did not mourn his loved ones lost.
By now the keepers of the sheep and herds
The ploughman steering his curvéd plough
All died,
Their bodies piled in squalid huts,
By poverty and sickness doomed to die.
On children's bodies, bodies of parents often lay;
And children breathing out their life
On parents' lifeless forms.
The plague streamed into Athens from the fields,
Brought by the sick and dying peasantry,
Who thronged within the walls from every part of Attica.
Every square inch of ground and every house they filled.
And so packed close in stifling heat
Death heaped them up in piles.
Many laid low by thirst rolled through the public ways—
Lay where they died, piled high around the public water founts,
The breath of life crushed out of them,
By too much yearning for a lovely cooling drink.
And everywhere through all the public roads and squares
Many you might have seen
With drooping limbs on dying frame,
Stinking and filthy, covered with rags
Wasting away, bodies foul,

(Text corrupt.)

With taut skin stretched over protruding bones,
Half buried though alive still,
By filth and squalour and by filthy oozing sores.
Again had death filled holy temples of the gods with lifeless folk.
Every sacred shrine
Was cumbered and befouled with lifeless clay,
Where vergers made a place for suppliants.
By now the worship of the gods, the awful power,
Counted for naught.
The press of present grief quite vanquished it.
The ancient rites of sepulchre were out of use.
The whole of normal life was broken up,
So every man in grief laid out his own.
The sudden horror, squalor, poverty,
Brought men to venture deeds unknown before, unheard.
Often they'd place their own beloved dead on stranger's pyre
And brawl and battle, even shed some blood,
To leave them there and then touch off the pile.

The notes in the Smith-Leonard edition of the poem on these final lines are worth quoting:

The whole ending of the poem presents a terrifying picture of the vanity of religion, of the belief in divine providence, and of the due performance of ritual. . . .

There is something utterly horrible about this final scene, the folk desperately scurrying about and fighting for the burial of their beloved—as if Death really did concern them—and preserving to the very end this one supreme and unrewarded pietas, *the concern for their own dead. The springlike radiance of triumphant Venus, which opens the poem, has wielded in the end to the awful will of Death. Such a conclusion would probably have appealed with especial force to a poet whose temperament is marked by a profound and brooding melancholy.*